DETOURS:

That Become Life's Path

Dr. Keena K. Cowsert

Foreword by Debra Talley

Detours: That Become Life's Path
Copyright 2018 by Keena K. Cowsert
ISBN 13: 978-0692159897
ISBN 10: 0692159894 (International)

DK Community Publishing
Keena K. Cowsert Press
PO Box 1642, Sarasota FL 34230

Email: DKcommunityG62@gmail.com

All rights reserved. No part of this publication may be reproduced, distributed, or transmitted in any form or by any means, or stored in a database or retrieval system without prior written permission of the publisher & author.

All scripture, unless otherwise indicated, are taken from the Holy Bible, New King James Version®. Copyright © 1982 by Thomas Nelson. Used by permission. All rights reserved.

Holy Bible, Kings James Version. Bible Gateway. Public Domain.

Cover Design by Dianne Steele Graphic Designs
Edited by Jeanne Bardel, Ann Gervasio & Rhonda Maalouf

Printed in the United States of America

ACKNOWLEDGEMENTS

I give honor to God, my Abba Father, who sacrificed His son for me; to Jesus who willingly laid down His life; and to the Holy Spirit who walks with me daily on this amazing journey.

To my dear friend, Debra Ann Talley, whose walk with Christ has been a testimony and encouraged me throughout life's journey. Thank you for always sticking by me and for encouraging me to finish this book, so other women can be reached and touched by God through the stories.

To all those who contributed their personal stories with such transparency. May God bless each of you.

To my friends, Dr. Tim Passmore, Pastor James Crockett, Mike and Ann Gervasio and Dianne Steele who reviewed this book and encouraged me that others would be touched by its content.

To Cameron Scott Cowsert for giving me some quiet time needed to complete this book.

To Dianne Steele for taking her time and talents to design the cover.

PRAISE FOR
Detours:
That Become Life's Path

Detours: That Become Life's Path will touch your heart! Through her own story and the willingness of others to share the painful detours of life, Dr. Cowsert takes the reader to a place of recognizing that Christ is able to provide healing in spite of the detour one experiences. At times, I found myself seeing my own detours in the lives of others, desiring to reach out and share in the hurt and healing of others, and longing to shout amen in the victory found in Christ. We all have experienced pain and disappointment in life. *Detours* provides a start or a continued path to healing from the detours of this life.

~ James Crockett
President, R1 Global Ministries

DETOURS is a true testament to God's faithfulness. This book is a collection of stories that show His grace and mercy. It will challenge anyone who will go on this journey, to find God in their circumstances. This is God's invitation to you, to follow Him on your *DETOURS*, to find an exciting and secure life in Him. Just open your heart, the journey is about to begin!

~ Debra Talley, The Talleys

PRAISE FOR
Detours:
That Become Life's Path

Life is full of moments that put us on unexpected pathways. Keena is very aware of this through her own experiences. As an educator, leader, counselor, mentor, and parent of several adopted children - she has seen first-hand how people react to these times of life change. Keena has an amazing ability to encourage others to have hope as she helps them understand that change isn't about defeat, it's about opportunity. I believe you'll find her words uplifting and encouraging.

~ Dr. Tim Passmore, Pastor
Woodland the Community Church

As I read *DETOURS,* I could not remain a spectator. The Holy Spirit spoke to me throughout, highlighting memories and hidden things. It is a book that happens to you as you are invited into an inner healing experience through a testimonials and reflection. You can feel the pain in each story. The impact of family sin, causing the derailing of lives – the "detours" that become journeys into victory because of the love and power of Jesus. The stories, scripture, teaching, reflective questions and prayer bring it home and become a retreat for the reader into God's healing presence. I could read *Detours* again and again and receive new revelation and healing each time.

~ Dianne Steele

FOREWORD

Dr. Keena Cowsert has been my friend, confidante, prayer partner, and sister in Christ for over 40 years. Whether she is in a counseling session, teaching in a classroom, leading a group of women in ministry, or dealing with a houseful of teenagers, her heart's desire is to see lives changed and drawn closer to Christ.

Of course, 40 years ago she wasn't "Dr. K." (She *loves* to be called that.) When we met, she was a 15-year-old girl and I was a 20-something young adult, just starting my career in gospel music. I had no idea that as a teen, she had placed me on a pedestal. I was also not aware of her loneliness and insecurity, because I was dealing with my own insecurity and self-awareness issues. After a few years, I announced I was getting married and leaving the singing group and Keena was very disappointed. She came to my wedding and I remember my mother saying that she had never seen such a sad face as Keena's at the wedding. Looking back, I think I must have been oblivious to her feelings. God had already started a lifelong friendship, but we had no way to know that at the time and were encountering our first "detour."

As life took us down different paths, we lost touch for a while. I thought of her from time to time, but had no idea where she was or how to reach her. While neither of us knew, God had a plan for our future. He brought her to my hometown to do training at a large company. She called and invited me out to lunch, and we started becoming reacquainted. It was somewhat awkward at first as our perceptions of each other were frozen in time. Neither of us knew what the other had been through, but we continued the building of our friendship, discovering the detours we each had been on and how we managed to find our way. For the past 15+ years, we have been the best of friends.

Our friendship and our lives have been filled with detours, but we have learned it is how we respond to the detours that matters, and we can choose. God's planned detours in our lives are placed there to draw us to Him. Keena and I both had those times early in life that could have caused us to spin out of control, but God was directing our steps to bring us into a deeper relationship with Him and each other.

This book starts with Keena's story and continues with the stories of women that God has put in her path. It is a true testament to God's faithfulness, a collective story of grace and mercy, and a challenge to anyone who will go on this journey to find God in their circumstances.

What if the detour *is* the journey? This is God's invitation to you: to follow Him on your detours to find an exciting and secure life in Him. Just open your heart, the journey is about to begin!

Blessings,

Debra Talley, The Talleys

TABLE OF CONTENTS

Introduction 3

Chapter 1:
    My Personal Detours 11

Chapter 2:
    The Detour of Sexual Abuse: Carol's Story 37
    Debrief 50

Chapter 3:
    The Detour of Secrets: Faith Grace's Story 59
    Debrief 68

Chapter 4:
    The Detour of Verbal & Emotional Abuse:
    Brenda's Story 73
    Debrief 92

Chapter 5:
    The Detour of Addiction: Bobbie Sue's Story 99
    Debrief 106

Chapter 6:
    The Detour of Rejection: Darlene's Story 113
    Debrief 120

TABLE OF CONTENTS

Chapter 7:
    The Detour of Physical Abuse: Marilyn's story ….. 127
    Debrief ………………………………………….. 136

Making Sense of Detours ……………………….. 141
    Verses of Encouragement ……………………… 142

Appendix A: Disease Model History ……………..... 144

References ……………………………………….. 151

About the Author ……………………………….. 155

Other Works by Dr. K ……………………………. 156

INTRODUCTION

INTRODUCTION

> *"I lay frightened in my bed, as a girl of age 12. I could hear my mother gasping for breath as my father choked her. They were just across the hall in their bedroom. I lay as quietly as I could and when I began to cry, I buried my face in my pillow so my crying could not be heard. I was frightened for my mother, but was even more afraid to try to help her . . . ."*

Many children go through similar situations, and live in silence and fear. This book is not about the silence, nor the fear. It is about these uncomfortable detours life brings. It is about the potholes and roads so broken-up, that a detour is necessary. The detours that come in life are those distinctly memorable experiences that seem both unfair and certainly, temporary. Those paths that we question and say, "Why do I have to take this detour - - this is not the way I wanted to go." While on the road, we still believe these detours are going to bring us back to the path in life that we believe we "should be on." So many injustices in this world. Things that should not happen, the loss of innocence, the loss of loved ones, and sometimes the loss of oneself.

How can one fathom the abuse, neglect, and abandonment in our world today? It may be parents that lose a child, the young girl raped by a family member, children that lose their stability through divorce, abusive words or physical violence. All these events change one's path in life. These are potholes or the broken roads that cause us to stumble and bring deep pain and scars. Surely, these events should never have happened and at some point, it will all be made right. In theory, this sounds good and it often gives us hope. Yet, the reality is that the detour often becomes life's path. Set on a course we may not want to travel, stumbling along the way.

This book will contain many stories of potholes and broken roads that led to *DETOURS*. These *DETOURS* ended up being a life path to a completely different place than could have ever been imagined. These *DETOURS* are much different from the "interruptions" you might have heard discussed by insightful people, such as Gloria Gaither. They are more than mere interruptions in life; they are a complete change to the structure of our path. *DETOURS* are paths we take that we believe to be temporary, only to find out they are permanent.

You may weep as you read these life-wrenching stories and then minutes later, find yourself smiling for those who have accepted the *DETOUR* in life as their path and have been able to make great things come from the seemingly impossible life situations. My prayer is that your life will be touched in such a way, that you may never be the same again. If you are one who is struggling with a gut-wrenching situation and are angry at God for a situation that is unfair and painful, I pray this book will give you comfort. May you learn to lean on God in faith and may He help you accept that the *DETOUR* is the path for your life. If you have lived on a *DETOUR* for years, searching for the way back, may this book give you a new view of your path. May you come to a place of acceptance, putting your trust in God to bring you out of the pothole and to place your feet on solid ground so you can move forward. Finally, for those of you on the other side of the *DETOUR*, looking back on the wondrous path God escorted you on, may you be able to carry this message on to others.

This book will take trips back in time in the lives of many adults. You will be reading the horribly true stories that may break your heart or may feel too familiar. Whichever the case, we will examine the *DETOURS* and the discovery of them becoming a life path. It has been said, "hindsight is 20/20", and we will be able to piece together God's bigger plan. We will be able to see how He has turned ashes to beauty, mourning to joy, and how He has restored life where there once was pain and emptiness.

Thus, begins the stories of those whose lives have been broken by sin and pain, often inflicted by the adults in their lives. These are the stories of the broken ones, whose lives can be healed by the Great Physician if they will give their lives to Him. These are true stories, written by brave women who now see the bigger picture. The *DETOURS* they took were destinies to other paths for their lives. More times than not, these were viewed as inconvenient *DETOURS,* while they were looking for the path back to the life they expected. You will see the struggles they went through trying to get things to be "right" in their lives and then you will see a point where they accepted their new path.

There may be moments at which you will scream and cry out to God asking why He would allow such horrible things to happen to children. There is a not an answer that will suffice except to say, "freewill." He gives us all a gift of freewill so that we can choose Him. Not everyone accepts that gift and uses it for good. Some choose to hurt others with the freewill they were given. You will feel anger toward many of these parents, yet many of them were hurt and abused as children as well, and the cycle of abuse continued.

As you read these stories from the young adults, say a prayer for them. The path for many of them is far from set-in-stone and they have much healing to do. They will be relaying some of what they have been through and the limited understanding they have of what it all means to them. Likewise, you will hear stories from some of the adults I encountered while working in Celebrate Recovery. Many of these brave adults are sharing, as they now have hindsight. They can paint a more complete picture of how God took what was intended for bad and used it to bring them to a new path in life. Remember, Joseph was sold into slavery by his brothers, and thrown in jail, yet God used it to position Joseph to save his people (Genesis 50:20).

Most of the names have been changed to protect the individuals. Others have chosen to use their real names as part of the healing process of "getting honest" and hoping their stories will touch other lives and give encouragement and strength. All stories will only contain first names, to protect anonymity.

While this book contains stories of other's lives, it is really a book about your life. You may be on a path you believe to be a *DETOUR* and you are feeling angry and frustrated that God is not doing anything. Begin a journal while you read this book. Write whatever you feel as you read these stories. No thought is unimportant or insignificant. Your inner healing may come, step-by-step as you process through your own thoughts and feelings. The Holy Spirit can lead you through a process of inner healing. God can take the hurts of the past when we are able to surrender them to Him.

At the end of each story or chapter, there are prayers. These are designed to help you to find words to ask God to show you things you may need to see in your own life. All inner healing comes through the Holy Spirit and He wants to see you whole.

Our journeys may look different, but we serve the same God; the one who can heal all wounds. May God comfort each of you in your areas of pain as we begin this journey through *DETOURS*.

> *But as for you, you meant evil against me,*
> *but God meant it for good, to bring to pass,*
> *as it is, this day, to save many people alive.*
> *Gen. 50:20 NKJV*

May God bless and heal you as you read this book.

Dr. Keena K. Cowsert   (Dr. K)

* NOTE - All references to satan will be in lower case - - I refuse to give him any glory in capitalizing his name. He will also be referred to as the evil one or the enemy.

Chapter 1:
MY PERSONAL DETOUR

Chapter 1: My Personal Detours

*But they that wait upon the Lord
shall renew their strength;
they shall mount up with wings of eagles;
they shall run and not be weary;
and they shall walk and not faint.*
Isaiah 40: 31

Detours in My Childhood

This story is probably like many others, but it is a story that must be told. I am a single adult, age 29 and holding (okay, I'm 50 something). In 2007, I stopped making excuses, and I stepped out and became a foster parent of eighteen teenagers over a three-year period. Nine of them became permanent through adoption& guardianship. For years, I desired to help teens, but kept making excuses why "I" could not do it. Let me back up a bit and tell you how the *DETOURS* in my life brought me to this life mission.

My parents divorced when I was ten. Both my parents remarried the same year and then began all the fun of two homes, four parents, eight grandparents, etc. I quickly learned, more was not better! This was a *DETOUR* I had not planned and did not want. I just wanted my parents back together and things to go back to how they were. As a child, it seemed like the end of my world.

Detours: That Become Life's Path

Divorce is never easy and it is often complicated by new blended families. My brother and I did not like the new situation. To avoid the situation as much as possible, I became a perfectionist at school, sports or anything I did. As an introvert, I would spend as much time as possible alone or with close friends. I just wanted things to be back to the way they used to be.

The first of God's provisions in my *DETOUR,* was on a weekend visit with my dad. My stepmother's family went to a Baptist church in town and on a weekend visit, at age 11, I accepted Christ. Had I not been on this unwanted *DETOUR*, I would not have been at that church that weekend and probably would not be writing this book right now. There is no way to know if I would have been introduced to Christ at another time in life or if I would have ever accepted Him through other means. The *DETOUR* had already made an impact that would change my life forever, but I could not see that at the time.

Salvation and all God brought into my life was an incredible gift during this difficult time. Not all my family shared in the excitement. On the weekends with my dad, I would learn and grow in Christ. At age fourteen, I went to live with my father and step-mother. The next two years would be a time of learning and growing in Christ. I even began attending a Christian school, which gave me an even greater depth of understanding about following Christ. At Christian school, I was learning and memorizing scripture that would prove to be a foundation for my entire life.

At age seventeen, things again began to change in my world and my life would face another crossroad that again became a *DETOUR* in my path. Over the course of a few months, several events occurred that began to open my eyes to who my father really was. I began to understand why my mother left him and that he was not the "giant" I had imagined. He was skilled at manipulation and lies and this tore my world apart. I had put so much of my trust in him and it was crumbling fast. He fled the state leaving me with my step mom. In the meantime, I moved back with my mom. The next few years were difficult and I had a lot of anger. Yet, I stayed in church and Christian school and did my best to live for Christ.

Detours in My Adult Years

The anger for my father and for other events of my childhood were deep inside me. On the surface, I was doing the right things, but I still had all this anger from feeling I was cheated in life by this *DETOUR*. Daily, the anger would manifest itself in sarcasm. This was my way of keeping everyone at a distance. Snide, hurtful comments that seemed harmless on the surface, but had underlying meaning. Trying to act all grown up, yet feeling like a hurt child on the inside. Not dealing head on with these issues lead me down another path, only this time, one of my choosing.

In my early 20's, my decisions lead me down this wrong path. It was that one small thing after another; I let my guard down and that allowed satan to gain a foothold in an area of my life. Because of the bitter divorce between my parents, I had become negative about the idea of marriage. I had told myself I would never marry or have children. As a result, at age 22, I found myself in a "safe" relationship that would keep that promise to myself - - I began a relationship with a married man. This led to heartache and disappointment, but it kept me safely away from the concept of marriage and children, which I viewed as the most painful of life options. This was not the course I had planned, but the road I found myself on. I chose this painful and unnecessary DETOUR! I came to a crossroad and I took a path that was not intended. It seriously affected my own self-concept, as I knew it was against God's plan for my life.

The constant disappointments and sense of being alone was overwhelming at times. Weekends and holidays were horrible. I had already lived with a dread of holidays due to the divorce and being shuffled around, and now I felt more alone than ever before. I managed to be a strong independent woman at work, yet in this relationship I seemed like a sappy, dependent female. Two years after the relationship began; I took a job promotion that landed me in Utah, a thousand miles from where lived. I moved several times over the next few years to Louisiana, Ohio and then to Tennessee. The relationship stayed intact through all the moves. I had become emotionally dependent on the relationship.

This negatively affected my self-image. I saw myself as a strong, independent woman and there was no way I was going to let a man hurt me or lie to me. Yet, here I was, in a relationship ridden with lies and secrets. As a teen, I had envisioned being in full-time Christian service and found myself on another path, far from where I wanted to be. The only thing going well in my life was my work. I was being promoted about every two years and rising the corporate ladder before even completed my degree. I had been with the same company for eleven years and loved my job. However, this too was destined to change. The day before Thanksgiving, my position was eliminated due to restructuring after a corporate takeover. I now found myself unemployed and again on another *DETOUR*!

Five weeks later, I landed a job as a regional training manager making thirty-five percent more than the previous job. This was a second time when God took something meant to harm me and used it for good. I was making more money and loved my new job. The position was in Nashville, which would once again move me away from this destructive relationship. Once in Nashville, I found a good church and decided I needed to move on from this relationship that left me empty and alone. I was desperately trying to find my way back to God. What I found was that the path away from Him took such a short time, while the path back seemed long and hard. God's forgiveness was instantaneous, but forgiving myself, took much longer. I had always envisioned myself in ministry of some type or marrying a pastor and I was a far-cry from that self-image. The internal struggle was difficult and the enemy fought to keep me in bondage. While things looked good on the surface, I was miserable! I was making good money for the first time in my life, but I still had not found my way to complete surrender to God.

Within two years, I had been offered a promotion and a move to Florida, which would put me near my mother again. Things seemed to be going well and I was making more money than I ever imagined, but I was not happy. Most of my time was spent on the road. I had become the South-East Area Training Manager and was responsible for twelve states and thirty-five trainers. My social life consisted of people I would meet in the hot tub at a hotel. That might sound exciting, but it is very lonely. I was now attending a church regularly and teaching a women's class; doing what I felt necessary to surrender my life to God.

The Upward Turn that Began Up-side-down

Then at forty, my life turned up-side-down. The entire human resource department, including training, was eliminated & outsourced as the result of our company being sold. Unemployed again! This *DETOUR* was not planned, but almost immediately, I was able to make sense of this path. My grandmother became ill that same week that I the loss of my job, which allowed me to be with her in her final months. The only problem was that she lived in Kansas, in the middle of nowhere and 700 miles from everyone I knew and loved. I accepted a teaching position at Emporia State College and four days after the semester started, my grandmother passed away. I had been privileged to spend the last four months of her life caring for her, which was a gift. Now, she was gone and I was left in Kansas four more months to finish the semester. This was not a *DETOUR* I wanted. Feeling somewhat alone, I had to rely on God to give me comfort and to be my source of strength. I was attending a small church (and I do mean small) that allowed me to draw closer to God during this time.

My Personal Detours

This *DETOUR* that seemed so lonely at the time, had placed me on a completely different career path. It took me away from Corporate America and had placed me in the world of academia. While a training manager, I had found that I was passionate about training and teaching. I did not really know my calling before this, but when I began teaching, it started to become clear. God had gifted me as a teacher and I was honing my skills to be a good public speaker too. The time teaching in Kansas allowed me the time necessary to take care of my grandmother's estate. When the semester ended, I returned to Florida and began teaching public speaking at a local college. I was teaching something I loved, and it gave me opportunities to share Christ. Based on our First Amendment rights, one can talk about religion or God in a speech. Isn't that cool!

Until this time in my life, I had been almost emotionless. Corporate America had taught me that emotions had no value. It was about surviving in a man's world and no sign of weakness could show. I now found myself, alone and grieving my grandmother's death. I was feeling sadness so deep that I could hardly breathe. I had never allowed myself to feel such sadness before, but now I found I could not control the grief.

For those of us who have walked the Christian life for any time, we understand the concept of the children of Israel wandering in the wilderness. They spent forty years wandering aimlessly because they would not follow God's plan. Here I was forty years old, feeling like I had no earthly idea what do to or how to move forward. God allowed me to spend two years in the wilderness, while he worked to change who I was and remove much of the past baggage I had been carrying.

God opened doors and I went back to school and began to pursue my Doctorate degree in Pastoral and Community Counseling. That may sound like a big deal, but school is school. I am sure kindergarten seemed hard at the time too. I felt God was leading me to write and author and felt I needed those credentials to do so. Thus, began this journey.

Two years after my grandmother's death, my brother died at age forty-one, as a result of alcohol and drug abuse. Scott had spent most of his life struggling with addictions and it had taken its toll on our family. Now his struggle was over. The saddest part is that I felt little over his death. In some ways, it was more relief than sadness. When he died, I told myself I would never again deal with another addict. Never say never . . . . .

God uses people to help us through the difficult times. He places them very specifically in our lives for those times when we need them. One special person in my life is someone I met when I was fifteen. Debra sang in a southern gospel group that came to my church. I thought she was the best singer ever (except for Barbra Streisand, who is the all-time greatest). Deb is seven years older than I am, so it was just enough for her to be a strong mentor in my life. As you read earlier, I had some tough things as a kid and listening to Christian records brought me some peace and joy. Yes, I said records – you know those big flat round things. For those of you too young to know what a record is, Google it on your iPhone or iWatch.

My Personal Detours

God places some people in our lives for a season, while others are for a lifetime. I had met Deb all those years ago and we had stayed in touch over the years. Then it was a casual friendship, which was mostly about me admiring what a great person she was. Then twenty years later, we were reunited in a much different way and grew into an adult friendship. I had moved to Nashville and she lived in the Knoxville area. She and her family were in fulltime ministry and spending time with them helped me to overcome my extreme introverted personality.

I can still remember the first time they invited me to go on the road with them and help over a weekend. That meant getting outside of my comfort zone, which meant not being in control of anything. It also meant getting on a bus and letting them see the real me for several days. That was a terrifying thought. What if they saw the real me and did not like what they saw? What if I got in their way on the bus? I had rarely ever stayed at someone else's home due to this anxiety and fear. I would happily entertain others, but would not accept invitations to other's homes. All kinds of anxiety plagued me and if it had not been for my love for this dear friend, I would have said a resounding, "NO." Yet, God knew that I would do anything I could to help her and her family and she was probably the only tool He could use at that time in my life to change me - - and I needed a major overhaul.

They would place me at their product table and make me talk to complete strangers! I was, and still am in many ways, an extreme introvert. Small talk and mingling with causal conversation was painful and senseless to me. I had been a manager for a Fortune 500 company and could communicate within that context quite well, including running meetings and conducting trainings. However, take me outside of an environment where I was in charge and in control, anxiety would set in. Business dinners were shear torture as they required small-talk.

Somehow, I survived that first weekend and then began to go on the road with them periodically. It was an incredible learning experience for me in many ways. It is always a great time of fellowship and spiritually uplifting. They are so incredibly funny (not sure they think so, but they are) and I learned to laugh – I mean really laugh - for the first time in my life. My need to be a perfectionist and serious about everything was slowly changing. I was finding a lighter and more fun side of myself. I also saw a family that truly loved each other and God. It was not that they did not have any disagreements, but that love was always present during differing opinions. Most of the stress on the bus was over what to wear and what to sing that night!

I also learned that I might not be the most stubborn person on the planet, which up until that time I believed to be true. Deb can match me stubbornness for stubbornness! It has become a competition to see who can win at things like, who buys lunch or who opens the door for whom. That too was a lesson for me, that I do not always need to be the one in the giving role. God gave me a friend with the same issue of not being good at receiving and He must be smiling as he watches us battle-it-out with His goal to change us both.

My Personal Detours

After several trips, I started to enjoy working the product table so much that I attended one big event for a week each year, and would stand there talking to complete strangers. God can truly work miracles! Being with a family that loves and serves God together was such a different experience for me, and something I needed to see and experience firsthand (Check out *The Talleys*).

God used many events and people over the next several years and begin changing my personality and I grew spiritually in ways I could have never imagined. God taught me how to cry, love, laugh, and mostly about how to have compassion. I had spent most of my life attending Independent Baptist churches and they had taught me lots of scripture and gave me a solid foundation in doctrine and for that foundation I am forever grateful. However, I exhibited little or no mercy for others. My attitude was kind of like, "you stepped out in front of the car, so of course you got hit - quit whining." You get the gist of my life? I loved God and wanted to serve Him, yet all the hurt from my past was keeping me at a safe distance from others. That way I did not have to love and possibly get hurt.

God led me to change churches to a large Southern Baptist church. I had come to believe that the Southern Baptist's were too liberal and worldly so this was a season of mental adjustment. There were many differences from the churches I had been in up till now. First, it was a large church and I had always been in small churches. People dressed casually, not in their Sunday best - - and Lord forbid, women wore pants to church. This church focused on outreach to our community as that was Pastor Tim's heart. If it was not centered in reaching or growing people, then it was not part of the church plan. God began to show me how to love and care for others at Woodland the Community Church. I had to let go of much of my past ideas of church to become part of this awesome group of people. I had to start focusing on how to help others rather than judge them.

Making Sense of the Detours

Many of the events in my life were now coming together to complete a plan God had intended for me. This began the process of accepting all the *DETOURS* in my life as God's ultimate path. At midlife, I am finally able to start making some sense of the things in my past. Each difficulty and *DETOUR* had been a training ground for what was ahead. If I were going to follow God and help others, I had to make some sense of all the craziness of my past. This began with my brother. Now that my brother was gone so was the headache of dealing with an addict – or so I thought. Remember, never say never.

A few weeks after joining Woodland, I was asked to lead a Saturday night singles group. I did this for two years and loved it! God began to shift things and one of the ministry leaders asked me to check out a program called Celebrate Recovery. When I found out it was an addiction recovery ministry, I said "No way – I am not working with addicts." God had a different plan, so once again, I found myself on a path I had not intended on taking, but at least this time, it was to follow a path God had for me.

My Personal Detours

Along with a co-leader, we began this ministry at Woodland church and for the next three years, and worked with addicts of all sorts. I learned that everyone has hurts, habits, and hang-ups that we need to work through. I had no idea all God would teach me or how it was preparing me for the times ahead. My brother's bothersome addiction helped me to understand an addict. This led to starting Celebrate Recovery and learning even more, not just about alcohol addiction, but many other struggles and difficulties life brings. During that same time, I completed all the course work for my doctorate in pastoral counseling and began work on my doctoral dissertation on addictions and 12-step programs.

This was also a time of great learning, not only about others, but about myself. I had the privilege to meet so many wonderful people on this journey. From a distance, some might look at the group and say, it was just a bunch of messed up addicts and on one level, they would be right. However, what it taught me is that WE ARE ALL a bunch of messed up addicts. Maybe not addicted to drugs, alcohol or sex, but certainly addicted to self and sin! If we are honest with ourselves, we each have at least one area that we struggle with most of our life. Some of us may masked it better than others do, but we still each have character flaws that plague us daily. The three years working with these very genuine and often transparent individuals gave me additional insight into the lives of addicts. Little did I know at the time; all the lessons were going to be used soon with teenagers who had parents who were addicts.

Detours: That Become Life's Path

Over the years, I had a deep yearning to help teens, especially those whose parents were going through divorce or just had a rotten life due their parents' decisions. God would occasionally bring to my mind a time as a teenager, when I heard Lester Roloff speak about his boys' homes in Texas. I thought how I would like to have a ranch one day and help kids. Now, this strong sense of needing to work with teens returned, but I kept telling myself, "Once I get married . . ., if I get married." I did not think I could do it alone, and that is true. What I was not factoring into the equation, was God.

Working with teens was something in my heart, but I would never have believed that I would have children in my home. God knew I would be taking in teenagers and that the ministry would be in my home. God also knew these teenagers would come from families with drug and alcohol abuse, from sexual abuse and neglect, and from some of the most horrendous situations. Little did I know that all that knowledge from my *DETOURS* would be used in the very near future with these beautiful teens.

One night in November of 2006, I was sitting in a restaurant alone (as single people do) and began to read a local magazine. I saw an article about the Sarasota Heart Gallery. It showed many children that needed foster and adoptive homes. It broke my heart! Two weeks later, I attended an orientation and in January of 2007, I began foster parent training classes. Each week I simply told myself, "I am going this week and we'll see." Each week, I became more convinced that this was exactly what I was supposed to be doing. On May 25, 2007, I was licensed and on May 26th, I picked up the fifteen-year-old girl (Jessie), whose eyes had drawn me in on the website. Over the next three years, I had eighteen teenagers in my home, each one that God clearly sent my way.

The teens God placed in my home all had parents with addictions. Most of the teens had been emotionally, and verbally abused and some had experienced sexual abuse asl well. All of them had experienced addiction in their homes. The scars and baggage they carried from their individual *DETOURS* in life seemed overwhelming at times. An inability to trust, anger and blind rage, poor social skills, and inability to bond or build relationships were just a few of the challenges that were present from day-to-day.

All the *DETOURS* in my life were now coming together to paint a perfect picture of God's plan for me. Each *DETOUR* I took on life's journey was an opportunity to learn things that I could now apply. While God never intended bad things to happen in my life or the lives of these teenagers, He was going to win the final round from satan by using each *DETOUR* and painful event for His glory and for the good of those whose lives I would encounter. While I believed, God was calling me into full-time service of some type, I could never have imagined it would be 24 -7 and in my home. My purpose at that point in life was to simply be there for these kids and to point them to The ONE who can truly help and heal them. There was nothing within me, strong enough or powerful enough to help these kids. God gave me strength, patience and wisdom each day to lead them toward Him. My role in the children's lives was and is to help them to break these cycles and trust in God. He is the only one that can heal the scars and pain.

God sent sibling groups into my home for permanent placement. There were other teens that came for several months at time and were a blessing in our home. Yet, God hand-picked nine teens to stay permanently. The first girl to come into my home was Jessie in May of 2007. She was fifteen at the time and had many struggles due to what life had handed her. One of her biggest struggles was just staying put! When the foster agency told, me she was a runner, they did not mean in the athletic sort. She had been running away from shelters since she was eleven. She was in out of my house about ten times and only lived with me for about nine weeks in total. Through it all though, she had memorized my number and would call me when she needed help. I loved this girl so deeply and it would break my heart every time she ran. I think God gave me the toughest one first to prepare me for what was ahead.

On July 31, 2007 God sent me two sisters, Miriam, age fifteen and her younger sister, age eleven who I will refer to as "Joy." I had to pray over this for a few days because I felt eleven was a bit young for me to handle. I felt God leading me to say "yes" to bringing these two girls into my home. With both parents in jail, they needed someone to count on. After some legal posturing, in February of 2009, they became members of my home through permanent guardianship. My life went from zero to TWO. For those of you who think we foster parents do it for the money, well when you take permanent guardianship, there is no money from the state to assist with their needs.

My Personal Detours

These sisters were loving toward me and I was very close to them. They remained in my home the longest of all the teens. They were very loving and mostly easy to have in my home. With each child, parents form special bonds and memories. Miriam and I used to wait for everyone else to fall asleep and sneak to the kitchen for a bowl of cereal. It was "our time" together. I miss those times! Joy was the most loving of all the teens. She gave the best hugs and never met a stranger. She would meet someone and talk to him or her for a few minutes and give them a hug and say, "I love you." What an open heart.

A few days after taking guardianship of Miriam and Joy, I adopted a sibling group of three -- Nadean, Nelson, and Rebecca. They had been separated from each other and in foster care for over six years. Nadean moved in (on her sixteenth birthday in 2007), followed by Rebecca and Nelson, eight months later in 2008. Then in February 2009, we found ourselves before a judge being forever connected through adoption. Nadean and Nelson shared the same birth mother, who they had been separated from since 1994, when they were three and two, respectively. They never had the chance to see her again and unfortunately, she died in 2004. Rebecca's birth mother died in 1998, when she was four. Their birth father had substance abuse issues and was unable to care for them. I was fortunate enough to become part of their lives. I connected with their dad and the kids began to rebuild that relationship as well. Now, my life has gone from two to FIVE.

Some of my special memories with them include: Nadean and I am taking a trip to Key West, Nelson and I would text each other from our rooms, and Rebecca, well she loves my dogs! She was also the last one to leave home at age twenty-one.

God had already been working on sibling group number three by bringing Cierra into my home in 2008. She had two sisters she had not been with for several years. We began to pray for her sisters, as it seemed that there was no way humanly possible they would be together. I began communicating with their birth mother who was in jail. Her parental rights had not been terminated and Cierra asked her to voluntarily submit her rights to allow her to be adopted. Her birth mother agreed and we planned Cierra's adoption and prayed for God to bring her sisters.

During this time, the older sister, Vennessa, had come to visit and wanted to stay. After going through the legal system to have her in my custody, she moved in. We were still in a battle for the youngest sister, who had been placed in permanent guardianship with a family that did not want her to see her sister, Cierra. After much prayer and assistance from the Guardian ad Litem office, we were granted visitation at my home. God had moved a small mountain to get this done! Once the visits began, it was obvious the three girls wanted to be together. God was going to have to move a very large mountain. It was difficult to understand how this family would want to keep her from her sisters. I guess I will never understand it. However, God moved in a mighty way and the sisters were all together. My life now moved from five to EIGHT.

Some of my sweet memories with these girls include: Cierra and I made a trip to Ohio and we had a great time.

My Personal Detours

Vennessa lived with me the shortest time as she was seventeen when she moved in. However, she went hard after God and that made our connection easy. She is also brilliant. You know how people say a person is a "rocket scientist." Well, her birth dad really was! He worked for NASA. And the youngest sister; well the funny memory of her is when the door knob fell off and she got locked in the bathroom.

During this time, there were nine other teenagers who came and stayed for various lengths of time. At one point, there were ten teenagers and six dogs and two rabbits in our home. Yep, it was a bit crazy, but the good kind of crazy.

Now to come back to that first young girl that moved in . . . At seventeen, Jessie had landed herself in a juvenile detention center. She had called me and I drove to see her six hours away. On one of my trips to see her, she asked me if she could take my last name when she turned eighteen. This really shocked me and as I made the long drive home, I wondered could this girl still want me to adopt her and give her a home? I wrote her and told her we would talk on my next trip up there. She did want to be adopted and so it took several people working together to get everything done before she turned eighteen. The adoption happened just a week before her eighteenth birthday. They had to bring her to the courtroom in handcuffs, let her change clothes in the bathroom and escort her to the courtroom. In January of 2010, Jessie became Skyla. Several of the girls changed their middle names or spelling of their first names, but Jessie wanted an entirely new name and she got it.

Detours: That Become Life's Path

During this time, I also took in my ten-year old great nephew, Cameron. He lived with us for ten months and then returned home. In 2015, at age thirteen, he came back to stay. Two of the girls were still living at home when he came. I would like to say the house is quieter now, but he is every bit as loud as the girls ever were. He is sixteen now, and has grown seven inches and three shoe sizes. He towers over me, but still knows who is boss - - - or so I hope!

We are still making memories, and some of the ones we have are a bit turbulent. Yet, the past five months he has grown up a lot (Thank you, Jesus). He is a hard worker and quite charming (when he wants to be). The biggest surprise this year has been his interest in Southern Gospel music. As I mentioned earlier, my BFF sings this genre and as a result I know several of the artists in that field. In February 2018, we went to lunch with some friends, Jeff and Sheri Easter. They are just good ole southerners. Cameron took to Jeff immediately! He rode on the bus with them to the venue and Jeff took him around introducing him to all the other artists. Now keep in mind, I have known some of these people for years, but they are hugging on Cameron like he is a king.

A local music promoter asked Cameron who his favorite group is and he responded, "da, the Talleys". Then he asked who his second favorite group was and Cameron said, "Karen Peck, of course." The others at the top of his list are Jeff and Sheri Easter, Brian Free and Assurance and The Hoppers. We went to South Carolina to another event in April and Cameron was working hard to try to get a group to take him on the road with them for a week or longer (like all summer). I heard him telling Bill Shivers, of Brian Free & Assurance, that they needed a product guy. Honestly, I could not have been more shocked at his love for something I also love.

The final count... TEN teenagers in my home. Now if you remember back to earlier in my story . . . I never wanted kids!!!!! Well, God had a different plan. If it were not for my *DETOURS*, I would not have been prepared for these eight beautiful young ladies and two young men.

> *". . . some have compassion, making a difference"*
> Jude 1: 22

The God Blessed Result

The paths we find ourselves on, due to the *DETOURS*, allows God to show us new things about ourselves, about Him, and about life. He rarely takes us on the path that we expect, but the outcome is so far superior to anything we could ever have imagined. One of my life verses is Ephesians 3:20, which says, *"Now to Him who is able to do exceedingly abundantly above all that we ask or think, according to the power that works in us."* We think we know where WE want to go for God, yet He gently leads us down a completely different path for His glory. WE think it is about what WE can do for Him, when it is about what HE can do through us. It is all God!

God never loses us, even though we feel lost. He never leaves us, although we might feel alone. He never hates us though we might feel shame. He simply loves us and offers us His mercy and grace to be with and upon us forever. Often in life, we are burdened down with the weight of the struggles and trials on our *DETOUR*. Yet, God is there! He knows our pain, for He endured it for us on the cross. When we feel the most desperately alone and broken, that is where God can meet us like no other. He can wrap His loving arms around us and give us comfort. There is nothing too big for Him to handle or too small for Him to care about. If we could simply see our *DETOURS* as a path where He is walking right beside us, maybe it would not be so frightening. One thing I know for sure . . . the *DETOURS* God allowed in my life were absolutely necessary to mold and make me into the person I needed to be for me to help the teens that God brought into my life. If we could just learn to trust His infinite knowledge, God could take us through the *DETOURS* much more quickly.

> *"As for me and my house, we will serve the Lord."*
> Joshua 24: 15

Allow yourself a moment in prayer.

Pause and yield to the God who loves you. Asked Him to show you the *DETOURS* and the paths they have placed you on.

Father, I asked you to show me detours in my life. I know you love me and only want the best for my life. Show me how to accept the path I am on and how to surrender my life to you.

SELF REFECTION

List some of the *DETOURS* God has allowed in your path.

What has been difficult about each *DETOUR*?

Have you seen good from any of the *DETOURS* in your life? Explain.

Use these questions to journal this week. Take time each day to write down the *DETOURS* in your life.

Chapter 2: The Detour of Sexual Abuse

Chapter 2: The Detour of Sexual Abuse

*If I say, surely the darkness shall cover me,
even the night shall be light about me.
Yea, the darkness hides not from thee;
but the light shines as the day; the darkness
and the light are both alike to thee.*
Psalms 139: 11-12

Carol's Story

"I felt like I was entering into the valley with death lurking all around me.

I believed if I opened the door to some things in my past, I would surely die."

I grew up the younger of two children in a family in St. Louis where I was violated by abandonment, abuse, detachment, and superficial family intimacy. My parents cast an enormous shadow in my life for years, both as a child and as an adult. I was always trying to meet my parents' spoken and unspoken expectations in an environment that sadly, would not allow anyone to flourish or succeed.

Detours: That Become Life's Path

To the world, we looked like the perfect family. However, we carried many untold generational secrets and an oppressive darkness permeated our household. It was not a place where a child felt safe or nurtured. It was a battlefield where you gingerly walked hoping not to step on hidden land mines. My mother, a high-powered executive during the day, turned into an abusive drunk by night. You could tell by the hour of day whether you would be facing mommy or mommy dearest. Threats were not veiled in my home, but rather were real and the punishment was severe and sometimes violent. This was my daily life and a *DETOUR* I did not ask for.

Since my caretakers were abusers, I had to develop an imaginary world by idealizing both my mother and father to survive. My need for intimacy and security was betrayed since I was sexually abused from the age of three to eleven. The mind is extraordinary with its ability to protect us by developing tools to help us survive. I developed an extreme phobia of tornadoes and constantly obsessed about them. I knew everything about their likely paths of destruction and the safest place to hide to escape their destruction. In truth, I unconsciously developed this phobia as both a ploy to divert my mind from the horror of my situation and to provide a reason to plead with my parents not to leave me home alone. They only laughed and chided me for being so foolish and left me by myself in a state of panic. The true reasons I panicked was when my parents left is because my brother would sexually abuse me. I now realize the tornado represented the shame and the guilt I carried and my belief I needed to be punished.

The Detour of Sexual Abuse

Unbelievably, with a strength and resiliency only God could have provided, I excelled in school. I developed a hidden belief that if I was good enough I would not be abused. I became an ultimate people pleaser – peace at any cost. The cost was me. I was lost with no sense of self and without a clue of what my dreams or aspirations might be. I was told what I should want and how I should feel. I was forbidden to show anger, yet everyone around me was raging. Deep within me was not anger, but rage for the injustice I was experiencing. It was buried so deep I did not feel it. I would later pay a high price for this unresolved anger.

My relationship with my father was a complicated one. I felt like a failure in his eyes because of his lack of interest in me. I now realize he had an insatiable desire for the approval of others. He was charismatic, affable, and adored by many. When others outside our family would speak to him, they would receive his undivided attention. When I spoke, he would respond in an irritated and demeaning fashion making me feel hurt and humiliated. However, there were those few and precious moments where he could be loving, sentimental and unexpectedly attentive. It was an emotional roller coaster, which made for craziness with both my parents. I felt like I was living in parallel worlds. There was a world of abuse and neglect, and there was the other world of merriment, laughter, and what I perceived as love.

I began suffering from panic attacks. This was another *DETOUR* I did not desire to walk through. I would feel like I was losing my mind and I would lie silently in my bed praying to God to stop them. They became a part of my life intermittently for some time. I used food as an attempt to masquerade a feeling of control in my life. I would alternate between depriving myself during the week and binging on the weekend. I lost the desired weight, but quickly gained it back when I resumed eating normally. I believed the deprivation of food was my need to be punished and the binging was like a child whose parent would give in to comfort them. Everything in my life went to extremes. I was out of control and only God could bring me back to sanity.

God's provision at that time in my life was a paternal grandmother who gave me love and hope. She was an amazing Christian who not only spoke of her faith, but walked it daily. I would often accompany her to church, where I would see her serve others with a joyous and caring heart. She added value to everyone who crossed her path. She cherished me and lavished love on me in simple ways, which would serve as an anchor through the storms of my life. One of my memories was accompanying her to one of the biblical movies of the day. Sitting as a child in the cinema, I was engrossed in the story of how Jesus gave His life as a sacrifice. When watching the scenes of His abuse, I would cry uncontrollably. I now understand that I was not only crying for the suffering He endured, but for my own as well.

In my early teen years, the sexual abuse had ended and I began dating in group settings. I developed a stringent set of rules to remove myself from temptation and protect my reputation. I wanted a chance to start fresh, without the stain of sexual abuse. I wanted to restore the feelings of innocence that I had lost. During the summer, before my senior year, I met my husband. As our relationship grew, I broke down and shared the secret I feared telling anyone. Derek was the first person in my life that I really felt a connection to and I hoped I might be able to trust him with the nightmare of sexual abuse. I expected him to turn away in disgust, especially since he knew my brother. His reaction was quite the opposite. He quickly reassured me that I was not to blame and he was angry about how I had suffered as a little girl. I marveled at how his anger was so present to him, while mine was not. It would not be the last time a person would feel anger on my behalf. The question was, "Where was my anger?"

We were married the middle of my sophomore year in college and left for what I loosely refer to as the honeymoon. This should certainly be the end to this long *DETOUR* in life and I should now be able to have a normal life. However, I was surprised when we arrived at our hotel and I was seized with a moment of terror that I could not explain. This was the man I wanted to spend my life with, but at the moment, all I wanted to do was run away. That night in a state of sleep walking, which had only occurred once many year before, I reenacted an event that I would later come to understand with God's help.

We set up house in New Jersey, but Derek decided on a job change, which landed us back in St. Louis. We experienced another *DETOUR* and had lived with my parents as we were attempting to gain financial stability. This made Derek uncomfortable since we were living with the ghosts of my past and the dysfunction of my parents' lives. One serious bone of contention was my abnormal desire to please my mother and father, forgetting that my husband was to come first. I felt like I was in a tug of war unable to separate from my parents and cleave to my husband as God commands.

We once again settled into an apartment and life resumed on a more even keel as I finished college. However, paradise was flawed by flashbacks of the sexual abuse, which hindered my ability to be fully present in moments of sexual intimacy. Our marital bed was not ours alone, we shared it with the ghosts of sexual abuse. It baffled me why this would now become an issue since we had been intimate prior to marriage. I felt like a failure as a wife since I could not be spontaneous, as I desired, since I never knew when these flashbacks would occur. I did not want to talk about it with a doctor and I tried to overcome it through mind over matter or simply living in denial. I ultimately found that until I dealt directly with the problems in my life, they would deal with me.

Life appeared stable until the rug was pulled out from Derek at work and we found ourselves in flux again. Derek decided to go to Dallas to pursue a new job. At the same time, my parents left for a two-week vacation, which left me alone in the house with my brother. I became increasingly anxious with thoughts of suicide, which lead me to a neighbor's home asking for help. I called my husband and he returned home immediately. After conferring with a doctor, he advised us to leave and pursue a job away from St. Louis and my parents, as it was an unhealthy place for me to attempt to heal. Thus, began the struggle with a chemical depression that would last for seven years. At times, I could function and at other times I would be totally dysfunctional. I had no idea how it would deprive my husband and future children of the wife and mother they deserved. At times, I felt like a house where all the lights were on, but no one was home.

It was during this time, I came to the realization that the world did not hold any answers for me. I was in search of something that would not fail me. The pain I felt was excruciating, yet there seemed to be no relief. It was the time my spiritual awakening would begin. I was unaware at the time, but God had a plan. A friend of mine from Dallas called me one day and said God had laid on her heart to bring me a Bible. I am so thankful she was obedient as I began to read it every night in search of answers. Just a few months later, Derek received a job promotion and we moved to Dallas. We began attending my friend's church and heard about having a personal relationship with Christ. My husband and I each accepted Christ and were baptized. Things began to improve in our lives and it seemed some of the pain was lifted.

When my oldest daughter reached the same age that I was sexually abused, I had a severe setback and was hospitalized for the first time. They were conducting shock treatments on me in hopes it would ease my depression. This *DETOUR* did nothing for me but erase two years of my memory. God always provided for my needs in his perfect time and this was no exception. Derek was attending a Bible study at the time and someone told him about a new psychiatrist in the area that was truly helping people. God orchestrated it so that I could work with this counselor. He began to work with me on the heels of my last hospital visit. This counselor believed that nothing was impossible with God. With the help of this anointed servant, my chemical depression lifted. He told me our time together was complete and that he believed I had received a miracle healing from God. He said if God had not intervened, I could have been hospitalized for the rest of my life.

My life had been returned to me, but I still had many lessons to learn. I became frantic trying to make up for lost time. I volunteered for everything under the sun. I returned to school in Chicago studying interior architecture and resumed therapy with a focus of the life as a child of an alcoholic and its collateral damage. However, at the same time I had become a driven mother of three who would put my own accomplishments before her family. I was a person addicted to the approval of others that was so engrossed in my own life that I could not hear my children or husband pleading for my attention. The sins of the past generation were now repeating in my life even though I held those behaviors in contempt as a child.

My salvation from the hell of myself was an invitation into leadership as a core leader in a Bible study. I was the least likely candidate for this role and as I was fearful and terribly introverted despite my desire to achieve. The thought of speaking in front of a group, regardless of size, paralyzed me. I was like Moses arguing with God that He had made an error by asking me to serve in this ministry. I

The Detour of Sexual Abuse

have learned that He delights in using someone like me to confound the world and to show that no one should boast in themselves, but in God alone. The other women who shared in Leadership became a support for me. They loved me unconditionally, never judging me or trying to mold me into what they thought I should be. Steeped in God's word and applying it to my life made all the difference. It was like planting seed, watering it and watching it grow. My life was changing. I now had a new voice and a heart that God had expanded with His love and my identity in Christ was returning me to my authentic self.

The next step in my recovery was the one I feared the most and was at my very core. I had dealt with the issues of my mother's alcohol abuse and its effects on my including the collateral damage my family suffered because of my inability to nurture and be present. I knew it was time to move on in my recovery when I received a phone call from a friend. She shared with me that a new group was forming for women who had suffered incest. I interviewed with the therapist and began both group and individual therapy. Many times, the most effective people in our lives are those who have walked in our shoes. I began probing into times in my life where memories were deeply buried. I felt like I was entering the valley with death lurking all around me. I believed if I open the door to some things in my past, I would surely die.

Sometimes, the pain of discovery can be so great that you will do anything to avoid it. Over the years, I had been plagued about an incident that I knew was not a dream, but I would not share it with anyone. I had prayed to God in my journaling that He would make it so apparent that I could no longer ignore or deny it. My answer came with a phone call from a former neighbor from my childhood years. She told me that she and her husband felt they should share something with me that they had hidden for years. This was the answer I had prayed for and yet, most feared. I believe we all know the hidden truths about ourselves and when we are ready to face them, God will reveal them to us and help us to face them.

Along with the night of terror, I had denied for many years, were also nightmares I could not explain. When I was ready to face the truth of what happened that night as a child, I finally saw the face of the man who was abusing me in my dreams. Sadly, it was the face of my father. Admitting this horrendous truth about my father was the hardest thing I ever had to do face in my life. God has mercifully not returned all my memories, but He returned those that have enabled my healing.

When people are severely wounded, their natural response is to withdraw and hide. There are many ways to run and some protect us as small children, in order to survive the circumstances, we find ourselves in. However, those defense mechanisms, no longer serve us well as adults. Instead, they become the walls that keep us from growing and achieving the true joy and peace that we desire the most. Jesus, as He did with Lazarus, called me out of my own cave of death. He called me into His light so the darkness could be dispelled and I could receive His healing. He has taught me the things that I must do to not return to that cave that held me captive for so many years of my life.

He has blessed me with others to walk with me on the road to wholeness.

My prayer is that we will all open our hearts to the ways that we hide. Places where our shame, fears, and anxieties prevent us from enjoying the true freedom that God desires for our lives. Our healing is accomplished as we find solace in God rather than hiding from Him. It is God's love that comes looking for us in our secret hideouts. May you allow God to give you people to come along side you and to assist you to grow and heal. May we all become restored, loving, imaginative and caring people. And may you find God and others walking with you as you come out of hiding and into His light.

> *For God has not given us a spirit of fear,*
> *but of power and of love and of a sound mind.*
> 2 Timothy 1:7

Allow yourself a moment in prayer

Pause and yield any memories that arise to God who loves you. Fear is no barrier to His love and power in your life. He is bringing up these memories for healing and greater freedom. Ask Him and Trust Him to do the healing.

Father, there are memories that I need you to help me process. I can have no fear because I have you. God, I asked you for freedom from these memories and the fear they bring. I trust you to do the inner healing in me. Thank you, Father, for the freedom you are bring to me now.

Detours: That Become Life's Path

If you have not yet received Jesus – Read the verses below.

<u>Romans 3:23</u> For all have sinned, and come short of the glory of God.

<u>Romans 6:23</u>   For the wages of sin is death; but the gift of God is eternal life through Jesus Christ our Lord.

<u>Romans 5:8</u>   But God demonstrates His own love toward us, in that while we were still sinners, Christ died for us.

<u>Romans 10:9</u>   If you confess with your mouth Jesus as Lord, and believe in your heart that God raised Him from the dead, you will be saved.

<u>Romans 10:13</u>   For everyone who calls on the name of the Lord will be saved.

<u>Romans 5:1</u>   Therefore, since we have been justified through faith, we have peace with God through our Lord Jesus Christ

<u>Romans 8:1</u>   Therefore, there is now no condemnation for those who are in Christ Jesus.

Ask Him to reveal himself to you and be your Savior and Lord.

SELF REFLECTION

Is there something from your past that haunts you? Write what you remember.

What are your greatest fears?

Where do the fears come from?

Use these questions to journal this week. Take time each day to write down your fears and what God is revealing to you.

DEBRIEF POINTS

Sexual abuse is a horrible thing to happen to anyone, but it is especially horrific when it happens to a child. Our world has become obsessed with sex, and this has led to 1-in-4 girls and 1-in-6 boys, being sexually abused according to Center for Disease Control studies (APA, 2013). This hideous thing that happens to a child is completely out of his or her control. The child is in no way responsible for or party to what is happening to his or her precious little body. It is a detour that is thrust upon the child; forever altering his or her life. At minimum, the child will have PTSD (Post Traumatic Stress Disorder) and it can even alter the child's personality. They are riddled with confusion, anger, and shame and left without an understanding of boundaries. This detour can never be changed – the altering of the path forever changes the child and the adult he or she becomes. The road for this child is full of potholes and broken roads, often for years, before returning to a somewhat better path.

Let us first look at the issue of incest/rape so we understand this issue from a statistical perspective. You may be one who is a victim of sexual abuse or may know someone who has. You may be completely naive to this issue and may well be confounded by the statistics. Once we simply look at the data, we will examine FEAR, as this is an underlying issue for those victims. Finally, we will study some ways God provides for us to overcome it on a daily basis. As you read this debrief, remember to use your journal to capture your own personal thoughts and feelings.

Debrief: Sexual Abuse

Understanding the Problem of Incest/Rape

Many adults tend to disbelieve, minimize, overlook or attempt to explain away allegations of sexual abuse, especially when it refers to child abuse. It is easier to ignore than face this horrid act. Children often feel responsible for what has occurred due to the absence of force (Rape Abuse & Incest National Network, 2009). The absence of force, does not mean the absence of coercion. Children of incest are primed by their abusers, through steps of coercion and secrecy.

In addition to incest, children are sexually abused by friends and neighbors. Nearly 90% of child sexual abuse victims know their abuser (Snyder, 2000). In excess of 50% of all rape/sexual assault incidents were detailed by victims to have occurred within one mile of their home or at their home. Here are some eye opening statistics:
- 4 in 10 take place at the victim's home.
- 2 in 10 take place at the home of a friend, neighbor, or relative.
- 1 in 12 take place in a parking garage.
- 43% of rapes occur between 6:00pm and midnight.
- 24% occur between midnight and 6:00am.
- the other 33% take place between 6:00am and 6:00pm.

Breaking down child abuse/rape: 15% of sexual assault and rape victims are under age twelve, 29% are age 12-17, and 44% are under age 18 (U.S. Bureau of Justice Statistics, *Sex Offenses and Offenders.* 1997).

Gender also plays a role in sexual abuse as girls ages 16-19 are FOUR times more likely than the general population to be victims of attempted rape, rape or sexual assault (U.S. Department of Health & Human Services, Administration for Children and Families. *1995 Child Maltreatment Survey.* 1995).

There are consequences from child sexual abuse that are inescapable. Some of these effects are that the victims are: 3 times more likely to suffer from depression, 6 times more likely to suffer from post-traumatic stress disorder, 13 times more likely to abuse alcohol, 26 times more likely to abuse drugs, and 4 times more likely to contemplate suicide (U.S. Department of Justice, 2012 National Crime Victimization Survey, 2012).

Overcoming Fear

Carol experienced sexual abuse that led to years of fear in her life. The fears came out in ways that seemed not even connected to the abuse. Our minds set defenses to deal with our pain and her mind allowed her to fear other things, such as storms and tornadoes. Psalms. 91:5 says, "Thou shall not be afraid for the terror by night; nor for the arrow that flies by day." The enemy (satan) thrives in the darkness. He wants to keep us in the dark, often using the memories of our past. If he can keep your mind confused and your emotions tied in knots, he can keep you in bondage. Carol had memories that haunted her - - memories that were unclear and frightening. The enemy may keep you feeling unrest and confusion about your past. He may bring terror at night and that darkness may bring fear. Sleep and rest may elude you at times. The ghosts of your past may be

Debrief: Sexual Abuse

ever-present in your today. You may feel as Carol described . . . that you are walking into the valley of death. Opening the door to face those ghosts may seem like facing death itself.

This is NOT what God intends for your life. God does not want you to live in fear. It may seem that all hope is lost and that everyone is against you. God says, fear not. "I will not be afraid of ten thousands of people that have set themselves against me round about" (Psalms 3:6). The bible says over-and-over again (365 times), "Fear NOT". It seems God knew this would be a major struggle in our lives so he tells us 365 times so that we have a reminder for each day of the year.

Could it be that God can see all the insecurities that feed our fears? Of course, He does, and He loves us anyway. He tells us, "Come unto me all ye that labour and are heavy laden, and I WILL give YOU rest" (Matt. 11:28). We allow our fears, our insecurities to weigh us down-- to drag us into the depth of despair with fear at the forefront. This is not what God has planned for you. He came to give us life and life abundantly. The enemy wants to destroy us, while Christ wants to give us life. "The thief cometh not, but for to steal, to kill, and to destroy: I am come that they might have life, and that they might have it abundantly" (John 10:10). He is the way, the truth and the Life (John 14:6). So how do we embrace this LIFE?

It begins one-step at a time. James 4: 7-8 give us those first steps. "Submit yourselves therefore to God. Resist the devil and he will flee from you. Draw nigh to God, and he will draw nigh to you." To have a life with peace, we must begin by submitting ourselves to God. This means to submit our thoughts, our past, and our present, to Christ. It may mean to stop dwelling on the past hurts. The enemy can and will use our past to keep us stuck. Have you ever tried to walk forward while looking back? At some point, you will stumble and fall because you cannot see what lies ahead while you are looking behind you.

One way to move from the past and to resist satan is to think on things that are lovely, pure, and honest (Phil. 4:8). Once we begin to transform our minds (Rom. 12:1), we can begin to draw nigh unto God. We do this by continually moving closer and closer to Christ by our actions. We replace old thoughts and habits with new ones. We fight our fears with scripture and faith in what God's word promises us. After we draw nigh, we can begin to abide in Him.

One of my favorite verses is Psalms 91: 1-2, *"He who dwells in the secret place of the Most High shall abide under the shadow of the Almighty. I will say of the Lord, He is my fortress: my God; in Him will I trust."* Rather than hiding, we should strive to ABIDE. I have read this verse repeatedly wondering, how do I ABIDE and where can His shadow be found. Some synonyms listed are stay, reside, dwell, and remain. Therefore, we are to stay where He is. We are to reside and dwell with Him. We are to remain even when we want to flee.

If you have ever watched birds in a storm, the mother will tuck the babies under her wings, protecting them from the storm that rages right in front of her. The baby birds are safe in the shadow of her wings. As long as they stay, reside, and dwell there, they will be safe. If they decide they know better than mom and wander out from under her wing, they will no longer be protected and will feel the raging storm.

When we feel, fear creeping in and stealing our peace and joy, we need to abide where God is. This may mean getting in a quiet place and reading scripture or praying. It may even help to pray or read aloud. The enemy cannot stand to hear the Word of God boldly proclaimed. It may take doing this over and over for the fears to subside, but they will if we are steadfast to abide.

> *He who dwells in the secret place of the Most High shall abide under the shadow of the Almighty. I will say of the Lord, He is my fortress: my God; in Him will I trust.*
>
> Psalms 91: 1-2

Chapter 3:
THE DETOUR OF SECRETS

Chapter 3: The Detour of Secrets

Whether you turn to the right or to the left,
your ears will hear a voice behind you,
saying, this is the way; walk in it.
Isaiah 30:21

Faith Grace's Story

My name is Faith Grace. I was born and raised in a Christian home with a large family, six siblings besides myself, and oh how I loved God with all my little heart. Family devotions were one of my favorite things to do in the morning, we would all gather around and read Keys for Kids, pray, and sing "read your Bible, pray every day and you'll grow, grow, grow. Don't read your Bible, forget to pray, and you'll shrink, shrink, shrink." At night, I would often go and put on my sister's silky nightgown and dance around to the worship music my mom always had playing. God and I were the best of friends.

When I finished the second grade, my parents felt the Lord was moving us to Asheville, NC, so we left Florida and moved. That is, everyone except my oldest sibling Michelle, eleven and a half years my senior, and my second oldest sibling Noel, ten years my senior, who were away at college. My time in North Carolina and the small private Christian school that God blessed us with is one of the most influential and memorable times of my life. I would never be able to explain how much I loved those people, that school, and the time spent there. The school was like family and Asheville instantly became home. My dad was a mover at that time, all over the US, and was constantly on the road; when he was near Asheville, he would stay there and when he was near Florida he would stay in our old house, where my sister Michelle still lived. For our summers and part of our winter breaks he would take us down to Florida for our vacation, so I got the best of both worlds. I loved my life. However, after our first year there, two of my brothers, Elijah and Richard, about six and seven years my senior, moved back down to Florida, and in with my sister Michelle, leaving me, my mom, another older brother Daniel, and my little brother David in North Carolina.

Since I was so young, I did not understand a lot of what was going on with Michelle, Richard, and Elijah. When I would go down in the summers, I started to get the feeling that everything was not exactly right with them. The worst part was that I felt they were not all that fond of God. I believed they would most definitely come back around. After a couple of years, when I was about ten, I finally got some understanding of what was going on from the event that happened next. My dad was down in Florida at the time and he called to give my mom some news. Richard had overdosed but they had been able to resuscitate him. Detour. Richard did drugs? Since when? What's going on?

That was just the beginning. Over the next couple of years, I tried desperately hard to adjust to this new turn or detour that I had now found myself following. It was so hard

The Detour of Secrets

though. Drugs, drinking, sex, parties, guns, fights...how was my family on this new path? We were all raised so right-- we had all truly loved God-- how did we get here? How did it go from me tattling on Nathan for saying shut up, to now worrying about my brothers stealing money from my other siblings for drugs? How?

About four months after Richard overdosed, came another bend in the road; my brother's best friend was murdered, and died right in front of Richard...*DETOUR*. Now one of my brother's friends is dead? Richard had to testify at the trial? Murder? How do I adjust to this? I am ten or eleven years old trying to wrap my head around this and yet it all just seems to keep spiraling downwards... until it finally hits bottom. I was probably around thirteen and in Florida for the summer. I was watching Tom and Jerry with my little brother David, when, the phone rang. It was my mom. She was crying, telling me that Michelle is being rushed to the hospital after going through a cardiac arrest and to pray.

We found out that the cardiac arrest was caused by accidentally mixing the prescribed Oxycodone, mixed with Xanax and alcohol. The doctors said that it was something of a fluke. I do not know how much time passed before I heard a car pull into the driveway. Looking out, I saw my sister Noel getting out of the car along with one of her old friends and her mother. Noel was just crying and crying so I am thinking she just got the news about Michelle being rushed to the hospital. She comes in and has David and I sit down on the couch. She puts her arms around our shoulders and asks me what I have heard about Michelle. I told her, then she looks at us, tears streaming down her face and in

Detours: That Become Life's Path

barely a whisper said, "Michelle didn't make it." I thought: Noel stop kidding. Then, I realized Noel would never kid about that. Michelle is dead...*DETOUR! DETOUR!*

I did not even know what to think. I prayed and screamed and cried out to the Lord. I even prayed that God would raise her up from the dead each day leading up to the funeral...just like he did Lazarus. But that did not happen. After the funeral, we went back up to North Carolina but mom decided that after we finished out the year, we would move back down to Florida. We had no idea there was still more to come in that year. About seven months after Michelle died, my closest aunt, my dad's only sibling, slipped in to a coma and died... *DETOUR! DETOUR! DETOUR!* God, how could there be more...how, how how? What is going on? Are you trying to kill off my family? Don't give me any of that "heaven needed an angel" garbage! What am I supposed to do? I'm just a kid! Why is all of this happening? I just turned thirteen for heaven's sake and everyone is dead, dying, and/or lost in drugs/alcohol. Not to mention, that I just moved from my home and all my friends in Asheville! And this was not even all of it.

For the first year after we moved I was confused and cried and did not really know what to do besides pray. However, after a year of that and God not responding in the way or time that I thought He should, I finally decided I was done. I was done crying and I was done serving a God that would let a kid like me go through all of this. At the age of fifteen, I was worn out and I was done. So, I ran from it all. I disclaimed Christianity and got in with kids that felt like I did. At the beginning, the people I hung out with just smoked weed and drank. One of them progressed more and more into drugs. He and I became very close even when he moved to another state. We would just talk on the phone every night for hours and MySpace each other until we were "dating". He eventually went from claiming atheism to claiming to be something of a Satanist and exploring witchcraft. What was so interesting was that while I was doing worse over the next year or two, my brothers and family were coming back together. Richard and Elijah were finding the Lord and getting back into college. In later years, after I came back to the Lord, Richard got accepted to the University of Florida where he graduated with his Civil Engineering degree and presently works with an engineering firm in Orlando. Nathan also got accepted to UF where he graduated with a degree in Building Construction and just got offered a job in Ft. Lauderdale. This proved the faithfulness of the Lord and His promise to turn all things for good.

Back to my rebellion. . . I was not doing so well. I had gone from my natural self, an incredibly happy, outgoing, tanned, blonde, sporty young woman to a withdrawn, depressed, suicidal, dark, moody person. I rejected everything that I was. I would not play sports anymore, refused to even go to the beach or get sun because I did not even want to look like that bright-eyed girl everyone knew and loved. I hated everything about that old me. Something I really despised and loathed was my name during that time. I could change my physical appearance, even change my attitude and beliefs…but my name…Faith Grace…it was like this constant burning brand that would not leave…a constant reminder that I was the Lord's. Little did I know that during the whole process, my family & friends were continuously interceding for me, & miraculously keeping me from drugs, drinking, and even protected my purity through all of it.

After about two years of this, the Lord broke up my circle of friends and I was suddenly left with no one to help fuel my rebellion. I was seventeen and so I found myself on a Monday night at a youth ministry, at the demand of my mother that I go there. I was listening to the woman preach and one thing caught my ear-- "burn your bridges". You see, I was tired. I finally had come to the decision that I was going to have to either kill myself or come back to the Lord. As it turned out, I did not have the "guts" to kill myself (the protection of the Lord but I saw it as guts) and I did not know how to come back to God. I tried a couple of times but I kept going back to my junk, so when I heard this word that you had to burn your bridges so that when you turned around to go back to the junk, it was impossible, because there was no way to go back. I knew what I had to do. I started burning bridges, though God had already gotten a head start.

Here I am now, I completed my Bachelor's degree at University of South Florida. Not to mention, playing all my sports again and spending time with friends at the beach. God has brought restoration to me and my family. So, at the end of all this, I want to leave you with some verses that help me with DETOURS in my life. I know I am young, in my twenties, and still learning more every day, but I just want to encourage you.

The Detour of Secrets

The Lord is behind, speaking and giving us direction. I do not have all the answers and since all that I wrote about, I have encountered just as intense and unexpected *DETOURS*. Do I have all the answers? No, I do not have all the answers, but let these verses bring you comfort. He is with you. A band by the name of For Today sings, "He is here; He was there; He is peace; He is faithful."

For You formed my inward parts;
You covered me in my mother's womb.
Palms 139:13

A man's heart plans his way
but the Lord directs his steps.
Proverbs 16: 9

Allow yourself a moment in prayer

Pause and yield any memories that arise to God who loves you. He may bring up memories for healing and greater freedom. Trust Him. The Holy Spirit may speak a word into your heart a word you need to hear.

Father, examine me. Show me things in my heart I have not seen before. Give me strength to face any secrets that have been buried. Jesus come into my mind and step into my memory and give me a vision of the freedom and change you want for me. Give me the strength to allow you to do inner healing in me now. Thank you, Father, for your healing touch.

Psalm 26:2   Examine me, O LORD, and prove me; Try my mind and my heart.

Psalm 44:21   Would not God search this out? For He knows the secrets of the heart.

Luke 12:3   Therefore whatever you have spoken in the dark will be heard in the light, and what you have spoken in the ear in inner rooms will be proclaimed on the housetops.

Mark 4:22   For there is nothing hidden which will not be revealed, nor has anything been kept secret but that it should come to light.

Psalm 19:14   Let the words of my mouth and the meditation of my heart Be acceptable in Your sight, O LORD, my strength and my Redeemer.

SELF REFLECTION

Does your family (or you) have a secret(s)? If so, what are they?

How have secrets in your life kept you from having peace and happiness?

What can you do to bring these secrets to light and move on? How will you draw from God for strength?

Use these questions to journal this week. Take time each day to write down.

DEBRIEF POINTS

Secrets are often the underlying cause of pain in our lives. "You are only as sick as your secrets" is a mantra of Alcoholics Anonymous (Lickerman, 2012). AA may have hit the nail on the head since one of the hallmarks of any addiction is deception. Addiction and secrets may be considered synonymous. Addicts deceive others to cover up their addiction and deceive themselves to deny they have a problem. Psychologists tell us that secrets can cause all sorts of emotional, physical, and psychological problems in our lives. It takes a lot of energy to bury a secret deep within us and while we think it is hidden, our body often tells us differently. Just as a parent can tell when a child is lying due to body language, secrets too can be seen in body language. Our bodies just cannot lie like our mouths can.

While there are many negative effects, there are reasons why secrets are kept. Secrets within a family can build cohesion for those holding the secret. The members view their secret as unique to their relationship. Bonding occurs when some family members withhold information from other members or the entire family has a secret they keep from the outside world. People hold secrets for a variety of reasons all revolving around self-protection. One may be fearful of disappointment, evaluation or judgment from other family members. Another form of self-protection is defensiveness, which is the fear of the information being used against him or her. A third form of self-protection is designed to maintain the relationship(s). The goal is to keep from harming the relationship and to reduce stress. A final

Debrief: Secrets

type of self-protection is simply for fear of retribution from an aggressive family member (Vangelisti, 1994).

Whether it is a parent or child addicted to a substance that they do not want the world to know about or a secret of abuse or abandonment; all the things we keep hidden takes a toll on us. The deeper we bury them, the more energy it takes to keep them hidden. We may think we have them securely tucked away, yet our actions and emotions reveal them. It is like placing a Band-Aid on a sore or concealer on a blemish. We may think we are protecting the sore or covering the blemish, yet neither will heal while covered. The sore needs air to form a scab and heal. The blemish needs to be clean, not all filled up with makeup. Neither will leave a scar if clean and exposed and over time they will heal. However, the more we hide or cover it, the more likely it is to take much longer to heal.

I cannot even count the times I told my teenage daughters to leave the pimple alone. Yet, they continued to try to pop it just to end up with a larger red spot on their faces. One of the girls had fallen and hurt her knee. She kept picking at the scab and I instructed her to leave it alone or she would cause it to scar. Well, of course mom knows nothing, so she continued to pick. Sure enough, she has a nasty scar of her knee and now when she notices it she will say, "Wish I had listened to you, mom". Just like the pimple or injured knee, we must acknowledge it is there rather than cover it and then, let time and nature take its course. If we try to cover it and interfere, it just festers and becomes worse. Only after we stop living a hidden life of secrets can the underlying pain or infection heal.

Detours: That Become Life's Path

God tells us that all things in darkness will be revealed in His light. God sees them even in the darkness - - He knows they are there. No matter how hard we try, we cannot keep them from God with band aids and concealers, He sees and knows they are there. He sees them and loves us anyway! He is waiting for us to reach out to Him for help.

> *For nothing is secret that will not be revealed, nor anything hidden that will not be known and come to light.*
> Luke 8:17

> *Let the words of my mouth and the meditation of my heart, be acceptable in Your sight, O LORD, my strength and my Redeemer.*
> Psalm 19:14

Chapter 4:
THE DETOUR OF VERBAL AND EMOTIONAL ABUSE

Chapter 4: The Detour of Verbal and Emotional Abuse

*"The Lord will guide you always;
he will satisfy your needs in a sun-scorched land
and will strengthen your frame.
You will be like a well-watered garden,
like a spring whose waters never fail."*
Isaiah 58:11

Brenda's Story

Church has been a part of my life, since I can remember. My earliest memories of church are from the age of four, when I lived with my mother and brother in Salina, Kansas. One Sunday after the morning service, I ran out of the hallowed, wood double doors with such enthusiasm that I smacked into the flagpole. Lying face up on the concrete, I heard the whipping of the flag and the clink of the chain against the flagpole. The brilliance of the noon sun blinded me, when I tried to open my eyes. Onlookers talked and laughed, abruptly bringing me back to reality. Reaching to feel the knot emerging on my forehead, I began to cry.

A man scooped me up into his arms. I was dizzy and disoriented but his gentleness calmed me. I pressed my face against my rescuer's chest and curled up in his arms, enjoying the refuge. A man's strength was unfamiliar to me as my father had abandoned us before my first birthday.

Detours: That Become Life's Path

This abandonment was the first *DETOUR* in my young life. Because of my father's own abandonment issues; he never developed the ability to maintain relationships, marrying many times and leaving several children fatherless.

"She's okay," my mother said as the man gently put me on my feet. I inhaled deeply, still in the grip of his aftershave. She clutched my wrist and jerked me towards the car. "Stop crying," she said, when we were out of earshot of everyone else, "You're okay."

In the backseat of the tan, rusty Ford station wagon, I rubbed my wrist where her fingers had left red marks. Tears rolled down my cheeks as I stared out the car window. "You just want sympathy," she said, as she glared at me in the rearview mirror.

I chewed on my bottom lip and tried to stop crying. My brother, John, turned around from the front seat and smirked at me. I looked at the blue Toyota next to us at the traffic light. Two pretty girls were laughing and bouncing to the rhythm of a song on the radio. They looked happy, and I wanted to be riding in their car. I rested my elbow on the open window and lowered my head. My heartbeat and forehead throbbed in a contradictory cadence to the music.

 My legs were slippery against the dirty vinyl seat. The humid air did little to cool my legs as the car picked up speed. Looking down at my ugly shoes, I picked up my left foot so I could see the bottom. I studied the heel; it was curved in a different fashion than regular shoes. The S-curve, rather than a C-curve was an indicator that I had flat feet - - *DETOUR* #2. The corrective shoes had an arch

The Detour of Verbal and Emotional Abuse

built into them so I could walk straighter and faster. Before I got the corrective shoes, my mother swiped my legs with a tree switch as we walked to the store because she thought I was walking slowly on purpose. These corrective shoes would start to define me in my childhood.

Our small family went to Salina Bible Church every service. I got a pin for learning my Bible verses, and a certificate "for regular attendance and faithful work" from Mrs. Phelps. Each Sunday I sat quietly in the hard wood pews like a good girl. Whenever I glanced down, I always saw the corrective shoes. The only color they came in was dull brown. I had to wear them until they were too small and so scuffed that the brown barely showed. I habitually crossed my legs at the ankles and bent my knees until the shoes were hidden under the pew. Sitting there, I mouthed the hymns. My brother's ridicule about my singing voice tormented me. I felt my voice was as awkward as my corrective shoes. Sometimes, I wanted to crawl under the seat and disappear.

One Saturday evening in May when I was five, my mother dressed me in a new pink dress, lacy gloves, and she let me wear my black patent leather shoes. My white ankle socks covered the broken skin and bruises left by the piece of wood she used to punish me with that morning. I had applied red lipstick to my new Raggedy Ann doll. I thought she looked beautiful, but my mother took Raggedy Ann away from me along with the play make-up, then beat me with the piece of wood. My sore ankles reminded me of my beloved doll that I never saw again. We walked to the Village Missionary Church that was close to Aunt

Ginnie's house. A slight breeze blew through my hair as my heels clicked on the brick street. Unsure what the occasion was, I pretended to be a princess on my way to a formal dinner.

A greeter at the church entrance handed me a small, red pamphlet and a name tag.

"What is this?" I asked.

"We're at a Mother-Daughter banquet," Aunt Ginnie answered.

The tables sparkled in the dimly lit banquet hall. I stared at the other girls and their mothers. The other mothers smiled at their daughters and kissed their heads. I was told to sit in the corner seat, by the wall. As the women at our table chatted, I continued my fantasy of being the princess at a party. I rolled a dialogue in my head, playing all the parts. Stretching out my arms, I pulled up the gloves, pretending to be royalty. These simple fantasies took me far from the physical, emotional, and verbal abuse - - *DETOURS* no child should have to bear.

After a dinner of baked steak, potatoes and gravy, buttered corn and warm yeast rolls, we had ice cream for dessert. Some of the women talked about me to my mother. I waited and waited for her to turn to me and say something. I wished it would be something nice like what the other mothers said about their daughters. But my mother never looked at or spoke to me until it was time to go. "Put your sweater back on," she said.

The Detour of Verbal and Emotional Abuse

The years passed, and each Sunday morning, my mother put on her church dress, applied lipstick and powder to her face. Muscles tense, I looked straight ahead as we drove in the same rusty station wagon to church. My brother's relationship with my mother was just as bad as mine, except he fought back with her both physically and verbally. I frequently became the victim of his misdirected anger - - yet, another unwanted *DETOUR*. When the frustration built up too much and he needed an easy target, I would soon feel the blow of his fists to my face, stomach, or any body part that got in the way. This happened almost every day. On occasion, he used my mother's antipathy against me instead of his fists.

"Mom, did you know that Brenda stopped in at that shoe shop you told her to stay out of? She was in there with Tracy, and she was talking to that man," he said.
"I thought I told you to stay out of there!" she said, "And I don't want you hanging around Tracy anymore. I don't like her. She's trouble."

I was quiet and nodded my head, but most of the time, in instances like these, we would get home and I would get the belt anyway. When my brother betrayed me like that, I was always tempted to take off my shoe and hit him in the head with it. Knowing I would get worse in return, I usually just bit my lip and stared at the back of his head. However, this time, surprising myself, I just screamed, "I hate you!" Suddenly, his fists were all over me and he slammed my head into the steel frame of the window. I saw flashes of light briefly before the pain. My mother glanced over her shoulder at me. "You asked for it," she said, pulling into the church parking lot.

Walking across the shell parking lot, I lingered behind, wiping the tears. As we entered the foyer of the church, my mother transformed into a terribly pleasant woman. On occasion, she stiffly put her arm around my shoulders as we sat in the pews. Her hand felt like fire burning through my clothes. I wanted to scream, "Don't touch me!" Instead, I shifted my body, so I could not feel the contact. I glanced at my feet. Earlier that morning, I had polished my shoes. They were still ugly.

Driving home from church, her biting remarks left no one unscathed. "She had so much make-up on, she looked like a raccoon. I don't know why the pastor's wife doesn't . . . Did you see what she was wearing?"
"What does it matter about some lady's makeup?" asked John.
"Well," mom answered, "she wears too much."
"You're an idiot, you stupid b____," John replied.

The fight continued the entire drive home. John's voice rose with each reply, his eyes bulged as if they were going to explode out of their sockets. The anger that brewed in our family often sucked in unaware casualties. Mom's distaste for life, us, and herself created a world of superficial fights. When we pulled into the driveway, I was emotionally spent and physically exhausted, even though I had not said a word. Mom did not forget the belt though, using the buckle for added emphasis.

The Detour of Verbal and Emotional Abuse

John was thirteen that summer, and it was then that he quit attending church. At the same time, I experienced a turning point in my relationship with God. Moody Adams hosted a revival at my church just as summer ended. Sunday through Friday, he preached for two hours each night. My mother and I went to every service and I listened intently, taking notes. I had never seen anyone like him. His pure white hair stuck wildly out at the sides, and his dark eyes sparked like struck steel. He explained the meaning of the use of numbers throughout the Bible and what they represented. On Friday, he autographed my Bible. He inspired me to read the Bible and pray often, and it was at this time in my life that the broken emptiness in my heart began its restoration. It was also around this time that when I looked down, I realized I no longer wore the scuffed corrective shoes. Shabby tennis shoes had replaced them.

Unable to reconcile in my head how my mother could read the Bible, go to church, and yet remain unchanged bewildered me. I slowly began to realize that the world she lived in was not rational. The rules in my home changed with her mood. If she did not scream and hit me, she punished me with silence. The fights escalated over the years to the point that the stress began to manifest on my physical and emotional wellbeing. Migraines would follow our screaming matches. My schoolwork suffered, and I began skipping school. One day after a fight, she sat in her chair, arms crossed with her face long and drawn. Her lips formed a thin line that I could not cross. I did not want things to be the way they were, so I knelt beside her chair and tried to talk to her. I apologized for whatever it was I had done. She did not respond. After half an hour, I began to beg and cry for her to talk to me. Giving up, I went back to my room and shut the door. I felt invisible. I pulled off my shoes and threw them at the wall. They bounced off the wall, across my dresser and onto the floor. There was something very wrong with my mother, but I had no idea what to do about it.

At fourteen, I got a part-time job washing dishes after school to buy necessities that my mother refused to. When school began that year, I found a different job that let me work a couple of hours after school, cleaning a day care. Each day, I walked the mile there, and began on one end of the building and cleaned to the other side. I cleaned the toilets, swept and mopped the filth the kids left behind. The teachers were very nice to me, except when they saved the clogged toilets for me. On most days, after I put the books on the shelf and vacuumed, I would watch the children climb into their cars and wondered what kind of homes they returned to. I found myself daydreaming about some of their families, making up my own version of the world for them, pretending that their lives were full of warmth and affection.

When I turned sixteen, a Rax Roast Beef was built down the street from me. Anything was better than pulling soiled toilet paper rolls out of toilets, so I applied and got the job. My first night at Rax was terrifying. They put me front and center as cashier. My fear subsided as the night went on and I enjoyed talking to the customers. The work was hard, but I earned money and made new friends.

The Detour of Verbal and Emotional Abuse

After work one night, I walked home to find the front door of my house locked; my mother had latched the screen door. I knocked but my mother would not let me in. She refused, and then demanded I give her forty dollars. I begged her through the dirty screen door to let me in. She called me selfish. Tired, shivering, and confused, I dug in my purse and pulled out my wallet. When she opened the door, I handed her the money. I went into the kitchen to get a drink of water, feeling her glare on me, colder than the night air. The grease on the bottom of my shoes from work caused me to slip and almost fall, adding to my embarrassment and fury. I felt like a criminal. It was two weeks later when I found out why she demanded the money. Our house had an oil heater that was planted in the living room; its unpleasant stench often permeated the house. It had run out of oil, but I had not even noticed how cold the house was.

John moved out that same year. I did not miss the punches to the face, or the constant bite of his criticism. With my mother working, and John gone, I had some peaceful time to myself. I spent hours reading books and writing stories. Propped up on pillows and barefoot, I dreamed of writing a novel.

During my sophomore year of high school, the relationship between me and my mother went from being a squall to a full-blown monsoon. Though my mother and I continued to go to church, we rarely talked. Anger was the only emotion she could express. Digging into scripture for guidance and comfort I learned things that I carry with me to this day. One afternoon when I was feeling especially alone, I felt a touch on my right shoulder and then Jesus whispered in my ear, "Everything is going to be okay." Like a warm blanket, peace enveloped me as I sat on my bed. Saying a prayer of thanks, I felt hopeful for my future.

There were a few people who took time out to talk to me, or just listen. Occasionally a rose would stand above the crowd. One Sunday school teacher, Phyllis, forged a friendship with me. When we talked, her brown eyes met mine. She had small metal framed glasses and short blonde hair that fell softly over her ears. She took me aside occasionally after class to talk. I told her about my brother's abuse, but I was not yet able to talk about the relationship I had with my mother. She looked me in the eye, and nodded her head. She did not say anything, and yet I felt understood in a way I never did with my mother.

"I am sorry you are having such a hard time. You need to know, deep inside you that you are special in God's eyes, and I think you're special too," she said. She then took my hands to pray with me. I left those Sundays feeling lighter. When I graduated out of her class, we continued our correspondence. She wrote letters to me until about ten years ago. She encouraged me as I became a wife and mother to always depend on God. When a child is abused or neglected, the attention of a kind adult can be Jesus with skin on. It is people like her that gave me a sense of value and the courage to go on.

When I met my boyfriend, John, I felt that I had been thrown a lifeline. I was sixteen and he was eighteen. My high school friend, Julie, set us up for a blind date. My trust

The Detour of Verbal and Emotional Abuse

in her had plunged after her first two set-ups. One wore chains, ripped jeans and would not stop groping me; the other became a stalker who came into Rax Roast Beef where I worked and without blinking he ate paper napkins dipped in ketchup.

The day I met John, I was walking my usual route home after work and a light breeze kept me from wilting in the warm sun in my blue polyester Rax uniform. I enjoyed walking; it gave me time to think. Cars sped by and I wondered what kind of lives those people were in such a hurry to get to. As I was about to take a short cut to my house, a white car pulled into the small parking lot where I stood. Julie waved from the passenger side window before opening her door. "John wanted to meet you," she said, walking up to me. "He couldn't wait until Saturday." From the back seat of the car, John stared at me. "He just broke up with someone and he is still hurting, just so ya know," she continued.

Great, another disaster I thought. John opened the car door and climbed out. His blonde hair glistened in the Florida sun. His nose and cheeks were sprinkled with freckles below his brown eyes. He held out his hand and introduced himself. Julie wandered around the parking lot so we could talk in private. Her boyfriend, Brad, sat with his eyes closed in the driver seat. I was grateful for having taken extra time with my hair that day, letting it fall into long brown waves. I wore my favorite brown/gold eye shadow with extra mascara that emphasized my hazel eyes. Usually shy with boys, for some reason, I felt immediately comfortable in John's presence. I studied the muscles on his arms and the way his white T-shirt was tucked in around his slim waist. We discussed the time and place for our first date and I gave him my phone number. There was a cockiness about John that both turned me off and endeared him to me. Giddy with excitement, I smiled the rest of the way home. I was not home fifteen minutes before the phone rang and it was him.

That Friday, we went to a party at a friend's house. I was shy, so my conversational skills were limited but I felt comfortable because my friends were going to be there. The sandals I chose squeezed and pinched my toes, but they matched my tight rust colored corduroys. Walking into the house, I scanned the living room, there was hardly anyone there, and the few people there had already become so drunk that they just sat on the couch watching television. John and I danced and talked in the next room. We asked each other questions trying to get to know the other. Less than an hour later, we decided to leave the party to go see the movie, "Conan the Barbarian." It was so bad we laughed about it as we left the theater. On the drive home, we stopped for hot chocolate at Dunkin Donuts. Just as John pulled out of the parking lot, a car sped towards us, causing John to swerve his Dodge Charger and spill the hot chocolate on his white pants. Our first date was a disaster; but I adored him.

My mother instantly began sabotaging our relationship. I came home fifteen minutes late from a date to find her sitting on the couch waiting for me. She instantly began to yell and threaten me, telling me I could not see John anymore. I collapsed on my bed in tears. Clutching the

The Detour of Verbal and Emotional Abuse

damp pillow, I fell into a restless sleep. The next day, I called John and told him what had happened. He did not understand her drastic measures but agreed to talk to her. We were both desperate to be allowed to see each other and the thought of not being able to, scared me to death. He was the only thing in my life that made sense. The next day, he went to my mother's work and asked for her forgiveness, promising to have me home on time in the future. To my amazement, she told him we could date again. However, no matter how diligently we obeyed her rules, she would find something to be angry about.

Every morning as soon as I was out of bed to get ready for school, she would begin to rant, screaming at me until I screamed back. With swollen eyes from crying, I would slide into my desk in first period chemistry class. Soon after, a migraine would begin at the back of my neck and creep up to the side of my face. The best I could do was put my head down on the desk and pray for the pain to stop. Because John and I were banned from seeing each other so often, it became routine for him to come to my bedroom window at night after he got off work and we would whisper through the window screen; other times he came to see me when I was on a break at work. Those moments saved my sanity. I believe my mother would have reacted the same way to any serious relationship I developed. Living in her world of toxic unhappiness, she certainly did not want me happy.

Around the same time, I hid a library book about birth control under my bed. I was curious about what the options were, but had no one to ask. My mother found the book

Detours: That Become Life's Path

and for two weeks she yelled, pulled my hair, and slapped my face. When I could not stand the torment any longer, I asked her, "What would you do if I told you we were having sex?" "I would throw the bastard in jail!" she shouted. And the next morning, in a hurriedly written note left on my dresser, she called me a whore and a slut. I could not breathe. I had to escape from her and that house and stop tripping over her wall of anger.

As soon as summer came after my sophomore year, I recruited my friends to help me move out of the broken, green house. At seventeen, I had emptied my savings of $250 to move into an apartment with a stranger from the want ads. Three days after moving out, I called my mother, hoping to hear in her voice what she had not been able to show me. Her response felt like a stab to my heart. "What do you want me to do?" she said. "Cry?"

If I only knew then what I had come to realize many years later, that my mother was incapable of love, perhaps I would not have wrestled with it and been tortured by this for so long.

John stayed beside me through the entire ordeal. He held me when I cried and loved me when I felt unlovable. He could have left my mess, but he did not. I finished my senior year of high school while working full time at Rax Roast Beef and maintained my own apartment. Because of my schedule, going to church had become rare. Even so, I knew Jesus was always with me.

John and I married the month I graduated high school. My mother refused to attend both my graduation and my

The Detour of Verbal and Emotional Abuse

wedding because John would be there. I scanned the audience the entire ceremony in hopes of seeing her face. At our wedding, my uncle escorted me down the aisle. Just as I began the walk in my new white sandals and summer wedding dress, I began to cry. I was happy for my new life, but still heartbroken from my mother's absence and rejection.

Already enlisted in the Army, John started basic training soon after. I moved into the Bradenton apartment his mother rented. We shared expenses and watched the television show, *Dallas* together. I started attending the church we had married in, Cortez Road Baptist Church. The people there were loving and friendly. I missed my husband, but I made friendships during that time that I still have today.

Once John finished basic training, I joined him in Oak Grove, Tennessee, next to Fort Campbell, Kentucky. We rented a trailer near the military base. Narrow and old, the rain sounded like hail on the tin roof. The polyester brown and orange flowered curtains were taken down and replaced with off-white ones I had made by hand. We were given a lot of hand-me-downs before we moved to help us get started. There was so much, I did not know where to put it all. I spent days sorting through it, not knowing what to use, and what to throw away. I became so overwhelmed one day I sat down on the brown shag carpet of the bedroom and cried. John came home and found me on the floor. "It's okay, just throw away what you don't think we'll use," he said, hugging me.

Detours: That Become Life's Path

The three years we were there, I slowly allowed myself to make choices. Being hundreds of miles away from my family allowed me to bloom. It was a time of new beginnings. I slowly began divulging my relationship with my mother to friends who helped me to clarify in my mind and heart that she had deep-rooted emotional and psychological issues. I began loosening the clutch my mother had so tightly entrapped me in, the one that told me I was no good and worthless. At first, making small choices for me felt peculiar; but my confidence quickly grew. Choosing what clothes to buy, or what soda to drink was liberating. I even bought new shoes.

After three years at Fort Campbell Kentucky, we came back to Bradenton, Florida, and began attending the same small brick church. John attended sometimes, but I attended often. I wanted to learn, but even more, I wanted to experience fellowship. My church family became my extended family. Realizing that the relationship with my mother would never be what I craved, my friends as well as my relationship with God helped me to fill the void.

I continued to labor through my issues and in doing so, a genuine healing took place. Working with the children at church was immensely satisfying. I taught elementary age children in Sunday school for several years. Seeing their eyes light up when I gave them fresh baked cupcakes made my heart happy. I traced their hands and made cut outs to paste on the wall each time they came. Eventually, their hands wrapped around the room in a big hug.

The Detour of Verbal and Emotional Abuse

Looking into their eyes, I recognized familiar pain. To those I gave extra hugs, telling them how special they were. I learned the concept of giving back. Looking down, one Sunday I noticed the beige high heels I had chosen to wear; they had a scuff mark on the toes. I smiled as I thought about how my life was changing and had changed. I had long ago thrown away those ugly brown corrective shoes. Without the difficulties of my past, I would not be the person I am today.

Over the years, I have made several attempts at having a relationship with my mother. I prayed often for guidance and direction. I craved her love, and still do - more than fried chicken. Unfortunately, she doesn't reciprocate my love. Our last time together, about twelve years ago, she walked into my house so full of hate it emanated from her in a palpable force. I was thrown into a fetal position on my bed, crying as the memories of hate and dysfunction filled my thoughts. That was the last day we shared anything, a word, phone call, or stepped into each other's house. Through Godly friends, Biblical teaching, and counseling, I have made peace within myself knowing that I have done everything God asked me to do regarding my mother. It took many years to work through the pain enough to know that I am not at fault. My faith has grown through the spiritual and emotional process as God filled the space in my heart left empty by my mother.

I may never know what is wrong with my mother until I get to heaven, I do know that I love her. I do not like her, but I honor her as God demands of us. The absence of parental love has drawn me close to the heart of God. He is my father and mother. I am so grateful for His love and mercy in my life. I would love to be able to pick up the phone and empty my heart to my mother. Instead, I pick up the Bible to seek Jesus' face in His word. My favorite is the power of prayer. I can talk to God like I talk to no other. I can be angry and yell or silent and rest in His presence. To those with one or both parents who love them, recognize your gift and pray often for them. While the "corrective shoes" and the *DETOURS* defined much of my childhood, God looked past the ugly scuff marks and rough roads and gave me hope and joy in life. He has and is making me brand new every day.

Allow yourself a moment in prayer

Pause and yield any memories that arise to God who loves you. The words spoken over you hold no power against God's love for you. Trust and sink into His presence. Allow yourself to visualize yourself in the Father's lap. He will wrap his arms around you. Can you feel His love? He will listen to you. Tell Him your thoughts and feelings.

Father, please remove the sting of words spoken over my life that were hurtful. Bring your healing to my heart and show me my identity in you. Let me feel your love and acceptance and let it sink deep into my soul. Thank you, Father, for loving me.

SELF REFLECTION

Have you experienced abuse and abandonment? If so, describe it.

Have you faced all your past? Did new things coming to mind as you read this story?

How does your past affect your present relationships?

Use these questions to journal this week. Take time each day to write down your feelings of abandonment.

Detours: That Become Life's Path

DEBRIEF POINTS

Many of you reading this have been through similar circumstances of verbal, emotional or physical abuse. It may have seemed at some points in your life as though the burden was too much to bear. The emotional scars live long past the stinging words, overly critical comments, and physical pain. The anger of the injustice buried deep within comes forth in anger, depression, anxiety, phobias, aggression, passive-aggression, avoidance, violence, substance abuse . . . and the list goes on. When the symptoms are expressed outwardly, it may be easier for others to see and for you to acknowledge; however, when the anger is concealed deep within your conscious or subconscious, denial of a problem is often the case. You might have lived for years feeling unsettled, angry, or anxious. Maybe you have developed phobias or have anxiety attacks and you are struggling to understand why.

Emotional abandonment occurs when parents do not create an environment for healthy emotional development (Black, 2010). The child feels they are not accepted for who he or she is. The messages they are given, according to Black, is that it is not okay to make a mistake, it is not okay to have needs, it is not okay to show feelings, and it is certainly not okay to have successes.

> The researchers behind the Minnesota Mother/Child Interaction Project followed children born to high-risk mothers from the time of their birth into adulthood. They concluded that children who had been exposed to hostile,

Debrief: Verbal and Emotional Abuse

verbal abuse suffered a host of negative consequences including poor attachment, acting out in anger, showing poor impulse control, and learning problems related to being easily distracted and having low enthusiasm (McCoy, 2009, p.98).

McCoy (2009) states that we are reluctant to label a parent psychologically abusive. Conversely, if a parent intentionally burns a child with a cigarette just once, he or she can be arrested for physically abusive. Yet, McCoy poses the question of how many times must a parent berate and belittle his or her child before we are willing to admit they are psychologically abusive? This inability to call it emotional ABUSE, leaves the child confused and feeling guilt or shame.

> Abuse in all forms affects us, yet verbal and emotional abuse often leaves us feeling abandoned by our abuser. Not receiving the necessary psychological or physical protection equals abandonment. And, living with repeated abandonment experiences creates toxic shame. Shame arises from the painful message implied in abandonment: "You are not important. You are not of value." This is the pain from which people need to heal (Black, para.1).

A child whose parent causes him or her to feel ashamed will lead a child toward a life of doubt in many areas (Erickson, 1963). It may result in a child being slow to interact or form relationships for fear of rejection. Interestingly, many of these children become adults and are still trying to gain the acceptance from this emotionally abusive parent as is seen with Brenda's story.

God does not want you to live in a place of guilt and shame, especially for things you are not even responsible for. He wants to give you freedom from this negative self-image you took upon yourself. God is truth and He says He knew you when you were formed in your mother's womb (Jeremiah 1:5) and He knows how many hairs are on your head (Matthew 10:30). You are so loved by God that He seeks you out; He woos you. He sees every tear you cry and hears every laugh too.

> *Who forgives all your iniquities,*
> *Who heals all your diseases,*
> *Who redeems your life from destruction,*
> *Who crowns you with lovingkindness and tender mercies,*
> *Who satisfies your mouth with good things,*
> *So that your youth is renewed like the eagle's.*
> *The LORD executes righteousness*
> *And justice for all who are oppressed.*
> Psalms 103:4

He saw the things that happened in your childhood and He felt your pain. Now, He wants to give you peace and joy to replace the pain and anguish. He tells us we can cast all our cares and worries on Him (I Peter 5:7). He will never hurt us, He will never leave us, He will be our Father, our friend, and our refuge in times of trouble. He can take the things in our past and create beautiful lives. He can take the ugly brown correction shoes and make beautiful feet if we follow Him.

Debrief: Verbal and Emotional Abuse

Before I formed you in the womb I knew you;
Before you were born I sanctified you;
I ordained you a prophet to the nations.

Jeremiah 1: 5

Are not two sparrows sold for a copper coin?
And not one of them falls to the ground
apart from your Father's will. But the
very hairs of your head are all numbered.
Do not fear therefore; you are
of more value than many sparrows.

Matthew 10: 29-31

Therefore, humble yourselves
under the mighty hand of God,
that He may exalt you in due time,
casting all your care upon Him,
for He cares for you.

Peter 5: 6-7

Chapter 5:
THE DETOUR OF ADDICTION

Chapter 5: The Detour of Addiction

Before I formed you in the womb I knew you;
before you were born I sanctified you,
I ordained you a prophet to the nations.
Jeremiah 1:5

Bobbi Sue's Story

I was born in Victorville, California on January 22, 1985. My mother and my father got married, when she was just a few months pregnant with me. My mother already had a son, Henry, and a daughter, Darcy, from previous relationships and I am my father's first born. A year later, my parents had my sister, Trish. My parents got a divorce when I was 5 years old. My mother left Trish, Darcy and me with our dad. My brother, Henry, already lived with his dad. I do not remember ever growing up with my brother. My mother and my father were addicts and partiers. This was my first *DETOUR*. My dad went to church one day and decided he wanted to change his life around. My mother could not accept this and did not want to change her life and so she left. So, my father was left taking care of three girls by himself ages 10, 5, and 4. I did not understand at the time, how she could leave us. This was my second *DETOUR*.

Detours: That Become Life's Path

When I was 7, my dad started seeing this lady from work. Three months later, they got married. We all moved into her place and started to live as a Christian family. My step mom did not have any kids of her own. She was a first-time mother of someone else's children and I am sure she was very nervous about that. We gave her a lot of problems and we were always in trouble. In my mind I remember saying, "I prayed for my mommy back, not a new one." When my older sister was 12, she was given the option to stay or go live with our mom. She decided she wanted to go live with our mom. When I was 9, my dad and step mom announced that she was pregnant. We were going to have a little sister, Taylor. This would be my step mom's first child.

When she was born, I believe Trish and I became jealous because of all the attention Taylor was getting. That used to be my attention that she was now getting. We started to cause more problems and get in trouble a little more. Losing mom was one *DETOUR*, but now having a step-mom and new baby sister was another. I did not like not getting all of dad's attention, which led to my next decision.

When I turned 12, I was old enough to determine if I wanted to go live with my mom. I decided I wanted to go and to Wyoming to "meet" my mom. I knew her, but not really. We only saw her a few times in 7 years. I remember making my decision because I knew she would not be as strict as my dad. In June of '98, I moved here to Wyoming. Everything was great. I got to use swear words and wear whatever I wanted. I could even eat whenever and whatever I wanted. I went from a set schedule and strict rules, to no rules and a very lenient schedule. My mom introduced me to smoking cigarettes and drinking alcohol before I turned 13. She told me if I became sexually active to just let her know so we could take precautions and prevent pregnancy.

By the age of 14, I was sexually active and by 15, I was pregnant. It was the beginning of my 10th grade year. In October 2000, when I found out I was three months pregnant. I knew right away that I wanted to keep the baby. The school counselors tried their hardest to convince me that adoption or abortion was the best decision for me, but I told them I did not want to hear what they had to say, unless it pertained to me keeping the baby.

I finished my sophomore year and a week into summer vacation I had a little baby girl, Justina Meloneigh Kay. I continued to go to school full time and worked part time at a pizza place. When that became tough, I talked to the school and we decided that I would go to school four classes a day and that would allow me to graduate with the juniors. I did that and started to work full time so my schedule never really changed. I decided to drop out of school half way through my senior year.

It was about two weeks after I had my daughter, when my mom called me into her room. My step dad was at work and the baby was in her swing. I went into her room and she handed me this light bulb and asked if I wanted some. I really did not understand what she was asking, so I asked her to explain. She told me if I wanted, I could take a hit off it. I was still confused, so she showed me what she was talking about. I asked what it was and she said, "Speed". It would help me stay up all night and give me energy and lose the baby weight I gained while being pregnant. She said I would not get so frustrated when Justina cried in the middle of the night because I would already be awake to take care of her. I do not know if I was trying to let my mom know that I approved of her or why I chose to do it, but I did. That's when my whole world twisted and turned into one big knot. I kept my job because it was not an everyday addiction when I started.

I married a man I worked with after being together for 6 or so months. Two months after we got married, he went to prison for a 4-8 year term. My daughter and I moved in with his mother for a little bit. I got our tax return and spoiled Justina and gave his mom some rent money. I got a job a KFC/Taco Bell and met another man. He seemed nice and at this point, I felt my husband was trying to control me from behind bars. The new man ended up being an addict too, which lead me deeper into my addiction. I ended up getting pregnant and I did not want to quit the drugs, so I did the one thing I was always against and had an abortion.

By the time my daughter was two, we moved back in with my mom. It contributed to getting us high all the time and it was just an endless cycle. My daughter never actually saw me get high. And I now know that even though I spent almost every minute of every day with her, I was not emotionally there. When she was 4 years old, I decided that something needed to change and that something was me. I confided in my husband that I needed help and did not know where to start. He suggested a lady he knew that could help with Justina until I got better. So, I met this lady and she seemed so right for the job. We wrote an agreement of temporary guardianship and she came and grabbed some of Justina's things and she was on her way.

My mother did not approve of my decision. She wanted me to give her guardianship, but it made no sense to me to keep my daughter in the same situation I was trying to get out of. My mother said I could not stay with her anymore, so I went to live with my dealer. He paid me to clean his house, while he was gone every other week. We only had a friendly relationship and nothing more. Instead of working on getting better, I ended up getting worse. I used the excuse of loneliness and my daughter being gone as a reason to keep using.

The lady who had Justina was letting me call and write and visit if I wanted, but once she realized I was not getting any better, she cut off all contact between us. I did not understand at the time and was furious and hurt. I started to hate that lady. I used even more by this time, thinking I had no hope at all, of getting my daughter back. That is when I turned to using needles.

In September 2012, I stopped and looked at my life and where it was headed. It was headed nowhere but in one big circle. My main goal in life was to get high and make it to the next day so I could get high again. That is when I decided to go to a church ministry program, Set Free. It is a Christian discipleship program for addicts of all kinds and who want to build a relationship with Christ. I was there for a month and realized I could do this with the help of Christ. The program gave me an idea of what I needed to do and I felt I could do it with Christ's help. I saw people who became dependent on the program, and I did not want to end up that way, so I left to do it on my own.

I have been clean for 2 years now and I could not have done it without Christ. I am engaged to be married and am working on trying to get a lawyer to keep my daughter in my life. I am in college and Christ has turned my life around. I do not want to rip her from the life she now knows, but I do want to be a part of it. I had to accept responsibility for the decision I made and work to build a relationship with Justina again. Life is not easy, but is it certainly worth living if done right. I will continue to rely on Christ and His help in rebuilding a relationship with my daughter.

Allow yourself a moment in prayer

Pause and yield any memories that arise to God who loves you. God loves you even when you make mistakes you wish you could change. He accepts you and His blood covers your mistakes.

Father, I am sorry for the choices I made. I know when I asked you to forgive me that you cover those mistakes by your blood and you remember them no more. Father, please show me how to forgive myself and how to rest in your love for me.

SELF REFLECTION

This story showed how drugs altered relationships. You may not have used drugs, but what choices you have made that altered relationships in your life? Describe them.

Looking back, what did you learn?

What are you doing differently now, to build strong relationships?

Use these questions to journal this week. Take time each day to write down how your relationships are working and growing.

DEBRIEF POINTS

There are many ways to damage or destroy relationships, yet since this story deals with substance abuse, we will examine that issue in more detail. Maybe the data included will be enough to discourage someone from taking that first drink or drug. SAMHSA's National Survey on Drug Use & Health tell us that 22.5 million people (8.5% of the population aged 12 or older) needed treatment for an illicit drug or alcohol use problem in 2014. Only 4.2 million (18.5 percent of those who needed treatment) received any substance use treatment in the same year (National Institute on Drug Abuse (2016, July).

The Cost of Substance Abuse

Drug use is such a prevailing issue in our society and is growing with the widespread use of marijuana. Of the eighteen teenagers in my home from foster care, all but one of those had one or both parents who were addicts. It seems that if we could eliminate drug and alcohol abuse, we could drastically reduce the number of kids in foster care. I would love to say we can solve this issue and protect our children, but our society is not doing much to eliminate or reduce substance abuse. According to the National Institute of Health, the economic cost to the U.S. is $193 billion (based on 2007 data) for illicit drugs and $229 billion for alcohol (based on 2010 data). This cost includes health care cost, crime and loss of productivity. It might be advantageous for them to add in the all the cost of foster care in the U.S. that is related to drug and alcohol use.

Debrief: Addiction

Part of the difficulty with eliminating this problem is that it is BIG business, both legal and illegal. The U.S. alcohol industry contributed $400 billion to the economic activity in 2010 (Distilled Spirits Council of the U.S., 2015). This includes the sale of the products, taxes on alcohol and wages for the 3.9 million U.S. workers. One can see why not much is being done to stop the sale of these destructive products.

One in every twelve adults, suffer from alcohol abuse or dependence and there are 2.5 million alcohol related deaths annually in the U.S. (National Council on Alcoholism and Drug Dependence - NCADD). No one ever takes his or her first drink and says, "I plan to be an alcoholic", nor does someone use his or her first illicit drug, hoping to be a drug addict. Yet, the numbers are staggering and users of drugs and alcohol are affecting their own lives and the lives of those around them.

Even more importantly, drugs and alcohol cost lives. According the National Highway Traffic Safety Administration (NHTSA), Traffic Safety Facts 2014 in 2014 an estimated 9,967 people died just from drunk driving related crashes, which accounts for 31% of all traffic related death and 290,000 were injured. According to MADD, there are 28 deaths per day due to drunk driving and every 2 minutes someone is injured. To expand beyond alcohol, the Substance Abuse and Mental Health Services Administration (2012) tell us that 10.3 million people reported to be driving under the influence of illicit drugs the past year.

Now that marijuana is becoming legal in some states, we need to look at this issue as well. Fatal car crashes involving marijuana use have tripled according to Columbia University's Mailman School of Public Health Report (WebMD, 2018). They report that one in nine drivers in fatal crashes tested positive for pot. In 2010, alcohol contributed to 40% of the fatal crashes, while drugged driving accounted for more than 28% of the traffic deaths. This is an increase from the 16% in 1999. Marijuana was found to be the drug to cause the increase, contributing 12% in 2010, over the 4% in 1999.

The Lie

Our culture has adopted a view of substance abuse as a disease. People believe it to be genetic or that there is an "addictive personality". However, research does not support either of these beliefs. These false beliefs came into existence based on cultural values rather than scientific evidence! If you are interested in reading more on this topic, see Appendix A.

The Truth

The environment, including family, friends, socioeconomic status and even quality of life, may be the most critical influence in determining drug use. "Factors such as peer pressure, physical and sexual abuse, stress, and quality of parenting can greatly influence the occurrence of drug abuse and the escalation to addiction in a person's life" (National Institute of Health - NIH, 2012). Once a person begins drug use, the drug(s) alters the brain making it more difficult to resist the impulse to take drugs according to the

Debrief: Addiction

National Institute on Drug Abuse (NIH, 2012). The brain is NOT altered before the drug use. There are many similarities that one can see with addicts, but they are all prevalent AFTER drug use.

The Bible also has several things to say about wine and strong drink. There are certainly warnings about the woes of alcohol.

Proverbs 20:1
Wine is a mocker, strong drink [is] raging: and whosoever is deceived thereby is not wise.

Proverbs 23:29
Who has woe? Who has sorrow? Who has contentions? Who has complaints? Who has wounds without cause? Who has redness of eyes? Those who linger long at the wine, Those who go in search of mixed wine. Do not look on the wine when it is red, When it sparkles in the cup, When it swirls around smoothly; At the last it bites like a serpent, And stings like a viper.

Isaiah 28:7
But they also have erred through wine, And through intoxicating drink are out of the way; The priest and the prophet have erred through intoxicating drink, They are swallowed up by wine, They are out of the way through intoxicating drink; They err in vision, they stumble in judgment.

Chapter 6:
THE DETOUR OF REJECTION

Chapter 6: The Detour of Rejection

*A soothing tongue
[speaking words that build up and encourage]
is a tree of life, but a perversive tongue
[speaking words that overwhelm and depress]
crushes the spirit.*
Proverbs 15:4 (AMP)

Darlene's Story

As I look down memory lane, a cold winter day in White Plains, New York stands out. I was eavesdropping on a conversation of my grandmother and aunt. You had to know the floorboards; to walk without them hearing the cracks and creeks in the floor. I had quietly walked close enough to hear their conversation. My grandmother and aunt stood, two tall, skinny black women with aprons around their waist. As my grandmother was making those corn pancakes from scratch, I could smell bacon sizzling on that pot belly stove. Oh, how my mouth watered for those pancakes. I heard my grandmother talking about my mother whose name is Mat Lee. Grandma said, "Mat Lee, should have gotten rid of IT." The IT she was talking about was me! The tears began to flow down my cheeks; as I heard how they called me names as stupid, dumb and ugly. Their voices changed as they spoke very bluntly about how they felt about me.

Detours: That Become Life's Path

They said I would never be accepted because of my father. My two brothers had the same father and grandma praised and gave hugs and kisses to them. I felt a burning in my belly, and then my mind felt like it was shrinking. I was trying to escape this pain that I felt deep within my belly. Was this true? Did the words spoken by the elders of the family contain truth about me? My life began on a *DETOUR* because of who my father was.

I come from a large family. Both my parents came into the relationship with children from a previous marriage or relationships. Now, my father was the step-father to four other children. One thing for sure is that I did not know who I was. My image of myself was not good. I kept many things hidden in my heart. Alcohol became my good friend, it numbed the pain. I struggled with the words that were spoken over my, life as a young girl being accused and rejected by my mother and her family. This spilled over until I was about fifteen, when I believe I had my first encounter with the Lord.

To find self-worth and escape, I joined the track team, and the summer Olympics, coming in first place in track, second place in tennis. I was always in competition with my niece as we were close in age. This gave me some positive feelings about myself, but my family's words would always come back to haunt me with a feeling of rejection. Whatever the women of this family said about you, became the label you wore. They were very domineering.

The Detour of Rejection

As a teenager, I had become outspoken. Members of the family would say, "Child just hush, no back talk". I stored it in my heart and I became cold and bitter. This developed into a look of meanness. My family had spoken deep seeds of curses over my life; by the words which they spoke against me. These seeds grew and caused my heart to become heavier with resentment. No matter how small the seed, it will grow. Words hold the power of death and life over the heart. My mom would say this cliché *"sticks and stones will break my bones, but words will never hurt me."* That cliché is a lie from the pit of hell. A broken bone can heal with proper treatment. A word released as a curse can bring a life of brokenness and abandonment, spilling into relationships and poor self-image. Finding the beauty in myself beyond the comments I had heard was no easy task. I had to recapture a love of my own deep within me. "What beauty?" is what I would often hear coming up from deep dark places of my soul.

Then, I met JP an auto mechanic. I had lied to him about my age knowing I was too young for him. A young man found me attractive and I was tickled pink. I did everything I could do so he would notice me. As time passed, he went into the service, we lost contact for a few years.

Then, I met Sam. My brother and his first cousin were married. His sister and I were friends in high school, although she graduated before me, we had continued our friendship and this is how I met Sam. He made me feel beautiful inside and out. His smooth talk pushed aside the doubts from my childhood, minimizing those bruised and broken feelings. As I was unaware of my identity, so was JP. This would eventually come to the surface.

He was more of a quiet guy, short in stature, shy, and a gentleman. On the other hand, I was loud, tall, skinny, and over-bearing. He would come to the school to pick me up with a proud look on his face. He walked with such pride as though he was a rich man. The fact that he came to the school, made my heart beat. My heart had never felt like this before about a person. I found out I was pregnant in my third year of college and married him. Things should have been good, but I had no foundation to understand what a good marriage or relationship looked like. As a result, I became abusive with him. I was dominant and spoke to him as I was spoken to; not realizing that he had feelings. During this time, Sam became an alcoholic, which made the abuse worst.

Sam and I have two beautiful girls. There was so much joy and love watching them grow up. We each began to travel to pursue our careers. Our careers became the Novocain to ignore what we did not want to face. We used our careers, just as many use strong drink to mask the pain, only to wake up in the same pain that now entwined me into deeper roots of oppression and depression. The travel brought other complications to our marriage, as we both engaged in immorality, as we explored unhealthy relationships outside our marriage. I began to date men that reinforced my negative self-image of fear and rejection. I knew eventually rejection would be the result.

The Detour of Rejection

After twenty-two years of marriage, we decided to separate. We both had begun to shut down. I built a wall so thick with all the adultery and drunkenness, I was losing my zest for life. As my self-esteem continued to plummet, it also affected my outward appearance. I reflected on the days of feeling ugly and my self-esteem dropped even lower. As if all this was not enough, I began to gamble after Sam left. Our home was in foreclosure and my job at the hospital ended in a layoff. I served Sam with divorce papers several times, but he refused to sign them.

After one battle of rejection, depression and fears of the unknown, I gave my life to Christ. I hung onto every word in the scripture on restoration for my family. But God's plan was different; I was to be restored, not my family. The Lord began to have me read about a heart of stone in Ezekiel for three months. This was preparing me to learn to open my heart.

In 2009, I was face-to-face with my fear. During our marriage, Sam had fathered a child. Our granddaughter knew Sam's 7-year-old daughter and invited her family on vacation with our family. My heart was cold, I was not ready for this illegitimate child to accompany me on my vacation. I was harboring unforgiveness in my heart for an innocent human being. I heard those words and relived those feeling that I felt when I was her age. I did not want to hurt her like I had been hurt. I repented. This girl said to me, "Can you love me like I am one of your daughters?" My heart melted and I heard the scripture in the book of Ezekiel 36:26 where it tells us of a stony heart made into flesh. This verse would cling to me for months until one day I let it change me. The love of an innocent young girl, began to work on me as I was reminded of what had happened to me years ago. All along it was not about me; it's about the love of God our Savior who died on a cross for me and you. He died for my brokenness, in which I do not have to suffer any longer.

I watched my heart melt in the hands of Jesus as He gave me a new outlook on life. My stony heart has now been transplanted into the heartbeat of Jesus, a heart of flesh. The little girl is now a young lady in her teens. Although we are not close, I am forever grateful to the Lord for a loving heart. I am beautiful, I tell my children they are beautiful, and tell my grandchildren how beautiful they are in Jesus. The mere essence of this story is that all children deserve to be loved. Love should not cost a child to bear adult guilt and shame as the enmity of one's heart is revealed.

Allow yourself a moment in prayer

Pause and yield any memories that arise to God who loves you. The words or actions against you have no power over you in Christ. Tell Jesus how you feel and ask Him to show you that your identity is in Him.

Father, I am the daughter of the most-high king. Show me how to live and walk as your daughter. Holy Spirit break the power of the words and actions from my past and teach me to walk in freedom. Thank you, Jesus for accepting me into your family and for seeing me as beautiful.

Detours: Reflection

SELF REFLECTION

This story showed how words or actions over our lives can leave us with a spirit of rejection. What words were spoken over you or actions against you do you remember?

How have those words or actions influenced who you are today?

What can you do to change any negative effects of these words/actions? How can you create positive words over others?

Use these questions to journal this week. Take time each day to write down how your words affect others.

DEBRIEF POINTS

The words spoken over our lives are so powerful. Even psychology, a secular view, can tell us about the power of our words and thoughts. This section will look at both psychological studies and the biblical worldview. This goes into data about how our brain works, so it is a bit more technical than past debrief sections.

Multiple research studies conducted by Masaru Emoto from 1994 – 2008, gives credence to the power of words. He took water and exposed it to good words and bad words, different types of music and to prayer. In all cases, the water crystals were changed by the interactions. The positive words made crystals brilliant in light and beauty. The water exposed to negative words and tone, became dark, muted and much less distinct and beautiful. The muddy and contaminated water exposed to prayer became lighter and more distinct in geometric form. Emoto concluded that our thoughts and intentions impact the physical realm.

Considering our body is more than 60% water, the question of how words impact a human became an area of study. Emoto showed how words change the make-up of water, so one would assume it would also change the make-up of a person comprised of mostly water. Those words influence our physical body as well as interacting with our soul, spirit and mind. There is a lot of research about how our thoughts and stress affect our physical bodies. So now, let us turn to the influence on our will and emotions.

Debrief: Rejection

Words that leave a child feeling rejection can inflict pain in many ways. Social rejection can influence mental, emotional and physical health (Weir, 2012). It increases anxiety, anger, depression, sadness, aggression & jealousy, while reducing performance on intellectual tasks and leads to poor impulse control (Dewall & Bushman, 2011). Williams, Ph.D. from Purdue University, suggests that those who are chronically rejected may experience severe depression, substance abuse or attempt suicide (Weir).

Words spoken over children often remain with them throughout their lives. They still hear the voice calling them "fat" or stupid" that may have been said by parents or peers. Even later, success in life cannot seem to silence the words spoken over them as children. Their self-image and self-esteem has been forever modified by these words without God intervening or potential years of therapy.

Research shows that just seeing the flash of the word, "no" for one second will cause a "release of dozens of stress-producing hormones and neurotransmitters. These chemicals immediately interrupt the normal functioning of your brain, impairing logic, reason, language processing, and communication" (Newberg & Waldman, 2018, para.1). Seeing negative words can cause you to become anxious or depressed and can damage key structures in your brain that regulates memory, emotions and feelings. Negative effects to sleep and appetite are also experienced (Newberg & Waldman, 2018).

Negative thinking leads to negative words, which become self-perpetuating and self-fulfilling (Alia-Klein et al., 2007). Negative words spoken in anger are even more damaging, as they send alarms from the brain interfering with the frontal lobe and decision-making center. There is then, a likelihood of irrational actions (Newberg & Waldman, 2018). Fear, real or imagined, has the same effect on the brain (Wright, 1995). Fear provoking words or threats will stimulate the brain into fight or flight mode.

The Power of "YES" and positive words on our lives is also something to consider. One would think the outcome of positive words would be immediate, but our brain does not react the same or as quickly to positive words (Kisley, Wood, Burrows, 2007). Research studies vary in the ratio of positive words to negative words. The lowest says you need three positive interactions for each negative one. Other studies say as many as 12:1. This is related to relationships (Gottman, 1993) and business (Losada & Heaphy, 2004) alike. Our positive thoughts and words influence the outcome.

The motivation centers of the brain are thrust into action with positive words and thoughts (Alia-Klein et al., 2007). A secular view of happiness by expert Sonja Lyubomirsky, suggests the more you engage in positive thoughts, the more happiness you will experience (Parks, et al., 2012). Creating a habit of positive thoughts also develops resilience when faced with life's detours and problems (Cohn et al., 2009).

Secular research aligns with Biblical principles the Bible teaches us about our words. It takes social science a long time to catch up to what was penned by Solomon, King David, and the disciples many years ago. We must be careful with words spoken to and over others, and we must be equally careful in the words we use about ourselves.

Biblical Look at Words

Proverbs 11: 9, 12, 17
The hypocrite with his mouth destroys his neighbor,
He who is devoid of wisdom despises his neighbor,
But a man of understanding holds his peace.
The merciful man does good for his own soul,
But he who is cruel troubles his own flesh.

Proverbs 15: 1, 4
A soft answer turns away wrath,
But a harsh word stirs up anger.
A wholesome tongue *is* a tree of life,
But perverseness in it breaks the spirit.

Proverbs 25:18
A man who bears false witness against his neighbor
Is like a club, a sword, and a sharp arrow.

Proverbs 18: 4, 20
The words of a man's mouth are deep waters;
The wellspring of wisdom is a flowing brook.
A man's stomach shall be satisfied from the fruit of his mouth; From the produce of his lips he shall be filled.

Psalms 36:3
The words of his mouth are wickedness and deceit;
He has ceased to be wise and to do good.

Matthew 15:18
But those things which proceed out of the mouth come from the heart, and they defile a man.

Matthew 12:34b
For out of the abundance of the heart the mouth speaks.

Luke 6:45
A good man out of the good treasure of his heart brings forth good; and an evil man out of the evil treasure of his heart brings forth evil. For out of the abundance of the heart his mouth speaks.

Ephesians 4:29
Let no corrupt word proceed out of your mouth, but what is good for necessary edification, that it may impart grace to the hearers.

Proverbs 16:24 says,
Pleasant words are like a honeycomb, sweetness to the soul and health to the bones.

Chapter 7 :
THE DETOUR OF PHYSICAL ABUSE

Chapter 7: The Detour of Physical Abuse

But as for you, you meant evil against me; but God meant it for good, in order to bring it about as it is this day, to save many people alive. Now therefore, do not be afraid; I will provide for you and your little ones." And he comforted them and spoke kindly to them.
Gen. 50: 20 - 21

Marilyn's Story

I was the youngest of five daughters born to a Baptist Minister and his wife. We were at church more than we were at home and I was raised with a strong Christian foundation. I am fortunate that my parents understood and taught all of us 'relationship' with the Lord. I credit my upbringing with how I handled my *DETOUR*. My plan was to be a wife and mother, to have a little white house with a wraparound porch and a white picket fence. When my children were grown, we would all attend church, hopefully together, and gather at our home for celebrations and holidays. That is not how life has turned out.

Detours: That Become Life's Path

In 1995, I met Ben he was charming, funny, generous, and proclaimed he was a Christian. In the first year, there were many instances of verbal and emotional abuse, but it took a devastating turn after our son was born. Ben had a daughter from a previous marriage and when our son was about five months old, his daughter, Amy came to visit. One day we were going to go to the zoo and on the way, we picked up some fast food. I told Amy to just give me her trash when she was done eating as I had the larger bag for trash; for some reason this did not make Ben happy. He threw my drink into my lap and, while driving, grabbed me by the throat, calling me every filthy name he could think of and threatening to kill me. He was so out of control he had to pull the car over and he turned around and headed home. All the way, cussing at me and shoving my head into my window.

When we got home he brought his daughter, Amy who was about 5 years old, to me and made me apologize for ruining her day. She went home, to a different state, and told her mother "Daddy is going to kill Marilyn." Over the next five years, there were many instances that mirrored this one with any spectrum of assorted circumstances. I left five times but was always wooed back with promises of change, love, and devotion to me our family and the Lord.

Two years after our son was born we had a daughter. When our daughter was 18 months old he did the unthinkable, he attacked me with her in my arms. Ben was self-employed so he worked from home. It was our son's birthday and I had gone to his office to tell him we were ready to sing happy birthday and have cake.

The Detour of Physical Abuse

Again, my timing was not good for him as I was about to find out. I returned to the kitchen with my daughter in my arms when he came around the corner grabbed me by my hair and dragged me into his office he pulled me up and threw me into the filing cabinets, my daughter was between me and the cabinets; as I begged him to let me put her outside the office he said "What kind of mother are you??? How could you put your child in the middle???" He beat me very badly and told me he was going to "Break every bone in my body and throw me into an empty well where I would never be found and if I was found he said he would come to the hospital and ask, "Honey who did this to you?"

I had no idea people hit other people so I felt this was somehow my fault. I had been isolated from friends, family, and even church for these five years so I had no one to talk to I was also ashamed of what was happening. Within the next few days, a woman in a public office saw the signs of abuse, thank God. She gave me the number to a domestic violence shelter and I left him the next week.

This was about 13 years ago when I took my children and left this extremely abusive marriage. I went into shelter on the East coast and traveled cross-country from shelter to shelter arriving in Arizona in July. After seeing my family, went back into shelter in Mesa Arizona. My intention had been to stay with my family but Ben called immediately after my arrival, which is amazing as it took me 30 days to make the journey (my car broke down in Amarillo) to Arizona. After about 90 days in a shelter in Mesa Arizona my children and I were accepted into a transitional housing program with Save the Family, an amazing program for survivors of domestic violence and homelessness.

My ex-husband however, is very wealthy and that has always left the scales unbalanced on many levels over the years. He had written into the divorce to pay me very little child support. I had a one-year no-contact restraining order against him. I was told if I attended the divorce hearing he could snatch the children from me as custody had not yet been established in the courts. I wanted nothing from him except to be left alone. He saw the children about 3 times over the next ten years.

Then three years ago, he wanted to fly them to Florida. My daughter was 12 and my son 15, and I felt they were solidly grounded in Christ. I could not have stopped him anyway; but I did find peace in their ages and understanding. They left in July of 2011; in August of 2011 I was in a horrible accident that shattered my kneecap. Being bed/wheelchair bound and in need of multiple surgeries and then therapy, I asked their father and his wife if they could help me with the children for about 6 months.

He immediately secured a high dollar lawyer and took the children and $750 a month in child support. I was unable to physically or financially fight him. That was the last time I spoke to my children. I flew to Florida last July only to be told they left the week before. He owns his own business; he sells hot dog carts on line and is a master at subterfuge.

One night in September of 2014, out of the blue, my daughter called me and I was able to get enough information to start making phone calls. They were in

The Detour of Physical Abuse

North Carolina and by communicating with the Haywood County Sheriff's Department and CPS I found out that my 17-year-old son is married, emancipated, and had dropped out of school. Ben had our son's phone disconnected and I have no way of contacting him. The police are unable to help me as when he married he became an adult.

My 15-year-old daughter is an atheist like her father. I know that God is bigger than this and she knows the Lord as her personal Savior. She has attempted to communicate with me however, Ben will not allow this and he has moved her, once again, beyond my reach. According to both the police and CPS, this was their father's doing. The situation is bad but Ben has covered his tracks legally. I have now filed a lawsuit, through self-help, as I cannot afford a lawyer, to get my daughter home. My son is beyond my reach but I trust the Lord will bring him home. I had no way of finding him. Both of my children are familiar with Save the Family and know this organization can find me.

I lost all my material possessions when I left Ben, then he took the children from me. One thing I know is God says in Genesis 50:20 'What man meant for evil, God means for good.' I truly believe that God is being and will be glorified in all of this. Naturally, I would have never chosen or prayed for any of these things to happen, but I have never been closer to the Lord than I am now. I experience the peace and joy that only He can give and it is truly amazing!

In August 2013, I accepted a position with Save the Family. I lived on-site at a campus with survivors of domestic violence and their children; facilitating wrap around services such as job hunting, community building, and classes. I am also interested in taking this to the next level and therefore I am back in school. When I was praying for God's vision for my life, I saw myself feeding homeless people. That could not have been further from what I wanted or was pursuing. In November, I had an interview to sit on the Continuum of Care Board (Coalition to end homelessness) here in Arizona. I had never thought I would be homeless, but I was, due to domestic violence. So, it was time for me to give back.

Then there was a turn of events! My son called me about a month after his 18th birthday and he was living in Virginia. He had been homeless since he was 16 and his dad kicked him out of the house. He was involved in drugs and living with a group of kids his age. He had just been fired from a fast food restaurant for eating off the line, he told me "I was so hungry and I didn't have any money." The way he was living was horrifying... he was terrified as he was in trouble with another group of kids over drugs. I asked him "Would you consider coming home?" and he broke down sobbing "You would let me come HOME?"

I booked a flight and picked him up at the airport on February 21st, 2015. I picked up a dirty, disheveled young man with a sheet full of his meager belongings thrown over his thin back...and my heart broke and soared all at the same time. When he walked in my front door he was greeted by my little Chihuahua rescue dog...he looked at her and said, "Keep that rat away from me!"...to this day this dog goes EVERYWHERE with him, he adores her and she taught him to love and trust again.

The Detour of Physical Abuse

He was suffering from PTSD to such an extreme that as we would stop at a stop light he would hide...fearing his dad was going to jump out of a car and a start beating him. He had been warned, "If you call or try to see your mother I will kill you!!" He would also dream that he came home and his dad was inside beating me.

He had started attending a trade school to become a car mechanic. I was so proud of him. He came home with a certificate from school and he proudly put it on our refrigerator. That night, he had a dream that his dad came in and ripped it up and physically attacked him. Every time my son would have one of these episodes, he would physically react as if it really happened. We went through a good year and a half of intense in-home healing.

The next two years had some difficulties in our relationship as I watched him struggle and heal. He now works as a manager of an apartment complex, he has a beautiful apartment. We are very close and spend several days a week together. More importantly, he has a relationship with the Lord that sustains him.

As far as my now 19-year-old daughter goes...I have not spoken to her. June 16, 2018, was a HUGE day! She flew into town from North Carolina to see her brother. She grudgingly agreeing to see me (at her brother's request) and I was reunited with her. I was excited and realistic. After my reunion with my son, I know that I should let her know how thrilled I am to see her without overwhelming her. I do know she feels guilty about her part as she does not understand that she had no choice. She lives alone or with various girlfriends and is estranged from her father. Prayers for her are coveted, and I know that this relationship will be restored to the glory of God!!

As for me, I am in a much better place. In June 2018, I received my Bachelor's Degree in Psychology/Life Coaching and remain the Regional Manager for a mid-sized property management. God is faithful in our *DETOURS* and in time, He heals the wounds and brings our families back together.

Allow yourself a moment in prayer

Pause and yield any memories that arise to God who loves you. The harm done to you has no power over you in Jesus Christ. Tell Him how you felt when you were hurt. He wants to wrap His arms around you and love you as a father should. Give Him your pain and asked Him to give you His joy.

Father, I have been hurt in the past but want freedom in my life. I have felt like I was unloved, but I know you love me. I felt unwanted, but I know you would leave the 99 for me. Jesus, you took my pain on the cross so I leave it with you now. I will not pick it back up. I asked for your joy in place of the hurt. I accept joy for mourning and beauty for ashes upon my life right now. Thank you, Father.

Detours: Reflection

SELF REFLECTION

You may not have been a victim of physical abuse, but is there something that the enemy has caused you to feel responsible for that was not your fault? Write what you remember.

What does God tell you about your past?

How can you rely more on God and rest in Him?

Use these questions to journal this week. Take time each day to write down your fears.

DEBRIEF POINTS

According to the Domestic Violence Statistics website (2018), every nine seconds in the US, a woman is assaulted or beaten, three women a day are killed by a husband or boyfriend, one in five teenage girls have reported a boyfriend threatening violence if they breakup. Domestic violence is also the leading cause to injury of women more than any other injury.

A woman who experiences domestic violence is often isolated from family and friends. Her partner will keep her from those that might intervene and this makes her more dependent on her abuser. Overtime, she will begin to believe the insults hurled at her and may blame herself for the abuse according to Refuge, a London based organization. These women experience anger, fear, shame, sadness, resentment and powerlessness. These lead to mental health issues such as anxiety and depression as well as physical illness, such as chronic pain, ulcers, problems sleeping and migraines to name a few (Office of Women's Health, 2018). There are also psychological effects on these women including, low self-esteem, lack of boundaries, memory loss, phobias, and many more according to the Final Report of the Task Force on the Health Effects of Woman Abuse in 2000.

Domestic violence is a serious issue for our communities as it has been reported to account for one third of the homelessness among families (Collinson, 2014). It has significant effects on children by creating threats to physical and emotional security. So, the fallout from

Debrief: Physical Abuse

domestic violence is seldom just felt by the women. Unfortunately, children are often affected as well.

There are ways to work to rebuild self-esteem but it is a process that takes time. Just removing the abuser from the situation does not mean all the damage goes with him. Some suggestions to rebuilding self-esteem are:

1) Create a list of things you like about yourself and add to it as new things come to your mind. Write down compliments others have given you.

2) Exercise daily! There is so much research that talks about the benefits of exercise as it releases endorphins to the brain, and lowers the chemicals that may attack an immune system.

3) Hang out with people who build you up! Positive people can be a great way to begin feeling better about yourself.

4) Seek Faith based/Christian counseling. This will help you to begin to see yourself as God sees you.... valued, beautiful and the daughter of The King.

5) Cut caffeine out of your diet. Caffeine has been shown to increase in the stress hormone cortisol, which has been associated with depression. These are just a few tips to get you started.

My prayer is that this few things will be useful for any of you that have experienced domestic violence.

MAKING SENSE OF THE DETOURS

Making Sense of The Detours

DETOURS come in all sizes and shapes, come at different times in our lives, and we may take the path alone or with others, but in all cases, *DETOURS* are unwelcome. They often come with pain and discomfort and last much longer than we would like. However, for those of us who are believers on the Lord Jesus Christ, there is HOPE.

God walks with us through every path set before us. Some are paths He places before us to take, others may be a path we chose, or *DETOURS* created by the decisions of others. No matter how we end up on the path, He will walk with us. I pray the stories in the book have given insight into your own life.
I hope the reflection questions and prayers have assisted you to find peace, freedom and joy through the Holy Spirit. I can think of no better way to end this book than with verses of encouragement for you to take on your journey! May God walk alongside you on the paths you choose and the *DETOURS* forged upon you.

May God bless and bring freedom and inner healing.

Dr. Keena K. Cowsert   (Dr. K)
DKcommunityG62@gmail.com

VERSES OF ENCOURAGEMENT

Deuteronomy 3: 22
You must not fear them, for the LORD your God Himself fights for you.

Deuteronomy 31: 6, 8
Be strong and of good courage, do not fear nor be afraid of them; for the LORD your God, He is the One who goes with you. He will not leave you nor forsake you. And the LORD, He is the One who goes before you. He will be with you, He will not leave you nor forsake you; do not fear nor be dismayed.

Joshua 1: 5
No man shall be able to stand before you all the days of your life; as I was with Moses, so I will be with you. I will not leave you nor forsake you.

Joshua 1: 8-9
This Book of the Law shall not depart from your mouth, but you shall meditate in it day and night, that you may observe to do according to all that is written in it. For then you will make your way prosperous, and then you will have good success. Have I not commanded you? Be strong and of good courage; do not be afraid, nor be dismayed, for the LORD your God is with you wherever you go.

I Chronicles 28: 20
Be strong and of good courage, and do it; do not fear nor be dismayed, for the LORD God—my God—will be with you. He will not leave you nor forsake you.

Making Sense of The Detours

Psalm 27: 1
The LORD is my light and my salvation; Whom shall I fear? The LORD is the strength of my life; of whom shall I be afraid?

Isaiah 12: 2
Behold, God is my salvation, I will trust and not be afraid; For YAH, the LORD, is my strength and song; He also has become my salvation.

Isaiah 42: 16
I will bring the blind by a way they did not know; I will lead them in paths they have not known. I will make darkness light before them, and crooked places straight. These things I will do for them, And not forsake them.

Jeremiah 1: 8
Do not be afraid of their faces, For I am with you to deliver you," says the LORD.

John 14: 27
Peace I leave with you, my peace I give unto you: not as the world giveth, give I unto you. Let not your heart be troubled, neither let it be afraid.

Romans 8: 28
And we know that all things work together for good to those who love God, to those who are the called according to His purpose.

APPENDIX

Disease Model History

The history of this model is important in understanding how it came to be popular (Fingarette, 1988). It is speculated that the disease concept may have originated in the 1800's from Dr. Benjamin Rush (Saint Jude, 2005). He used this idea to promote the prohibitionist platforms, which lead to the temperance movement. The temperance movement was successful in 1919 when the Eighteenth Amendment to the Constitution was ratified prohibiting the production, transportation, or sale of liquors. Alcohol-related illness declined during the 1920's. In 1933, the Prohibition was repealed. In 1935, the Oxford Group, which consisted of four members, formed AA. The belief of the disease model was derived from their ideas that drinking was a symptom of a disease (Fingarette; Marron, 1993).

Shortly after, Jellinek, a research professor in Applied Physiology at Yale University, published two articles in 1946 and 1952, which were funded by Marty Mann, an AA member. Jellinek's landmark work was based on questionnaires designed by AA and distributed by AA to its membership. These findings were based on questionnaires completed by 98 male members of AA. Jellinek excluded those filled out by women because their data differed from the men's data. Jellinek recognized some limitations based on the survey participants, and cautioned his readers about the limited nature of his data (Fingarette, 1988). From this research, Jellinek developed a basic pattern or sequence of phases that resembled the AA disease model.

In the 1960s, several national studies conflicted with Jellinek's sequence of phases. Jellinek's response was an acknowledgement the lack of a scientific foundation and remarked on his lack of evidence by stating; "For the time being this may suffice, but not indefinitely" (Jellinek, 1960, p. 159). Yale even asked him to refute his own findings, which he did and the "stages of alcoholism he had identified did not stand up to scientific scrutiny" (Saint Jude, 2005, ¶16).). However, the treatment of alcoholism had become big business with political power, such as the National Council on Alcoholism (NCA), which was founded by Marty Mann (e.g. Wiener, 1981; Olson & Gerstein, 1985). Mann used her position to promote the disease model (Saint Jude, 2005). Additionally, Smithers who funded Jellinek's work and supported the disease model, also founded the National Institute for Alcoholism and Alcohol Abuse (NIAAA), and used this as a platform to promote the disease model (Saint Jude, 2005).

Another interesting facet of this discussion is that many of those working in the 12-step field are simply paraprofessional, without the benefit of scientific or professional training (Fingarette, 1988). "Paraprofessional often see empirical scientific data as obscure, irrelevant, or contradictory to their personal experiential knowledge of alcoholism" (Vaillant, 1983, p. 20). Personal knowledge has become ingrained due to what members were being told at AA.

The NIAAA, which funds 90 percent of the U.S. research on alcoholism, states that scientist are searching for the genetic link that increases the risk of alcoholism (DHHS, 2004b). However, no such gene has been found. Despite the lack of empirical research, the disease model has become integrated in the US culture (Fingarette, 1988). These overriding views are neither scientific nor rational (Marron, 1993). Thus, the myth is of alcoholism as a disease is born, and is carried on from generation to generation. The results and implications of Jellinek's studies and AA's strong presence was an effort to get the medical community to recognize and treat substance abuse and dependence.

Implications. In 1956, the American Medical Association (AMA) called for alcoholism to be treated as a disease by the medical community (Merta, 2001). Upon review, the AMA website does not offer any data providing sound reasoning for classifying alcoholism (drug dependence) as a disease. The AMA website identifies three definitions: (a) alcoholism as a disability (J-30.995); (b) drug dependencies as diseases (H-95.983); and (c) dual disease classification of alcoholism (H-30.997), which states it is both psychiatric and medical. According to H-30.997, the AMA "affirms that individuals who suffer from drug addiction in any of its manifestations are persons with a treatable disease" (no. 4). Two additional policies, H-30.983 and H-300.962, deal with medical education and the practice of addiction medicine. The "AMA policy states that alcohol and other drug abuse education needs to be an integral part of medical education" (Res. 303, I-94). The purpose of these definitions was to classify and code the disorder so it could be recognized and treated by the medical community.

The *American Medical Association Complete Medical Encyclopedia* (2003) contains sections on drug addiction, which can be viewed online at the AMA Medical Library website. As seen below, this section does not refer to drug addiction as a disease.

> Drug addiction is a disorder involving physical and psychological dependence on a drug or drugs and characterized by tolerance (the need to consume larger and larger amounts of the drug to feel its effects), physical symptoms if the drug is withdrawn, or both. Drug addiction poses serious

health risks because of its long-term physical effects, disruption of family and work life, and the symptoms of drug withdrawal, which can range from highly unpleasant to fatal. In most cases, the disorder begins as drug abuse – the use of illegal drugs, or the use of a legal drug in excessive quantities or for purposes other than those for which it is intended – and progresses over time into addiction. (¶ 1)

In addition, the AMA called for Congress and others to work to stop underage drinking in September of 2003. A year later, in September of 2004, the AMA published an article revealing the deduction of alcohol-related problems at colleges. Both articles seem to deny the diseases model by the very nature of their existence. If alcohol dependence is a disease, then an individual is both prone to have it and can do little if anything to stop its onset, meaning it is involuntary (Schaler, 2000). The AMA articles validate the position that drinking is a choice and that laws and social programs can be put in place to reduce alcohol dependence and abuse from the AMA's own words.

When viewing the government National Institute of Health (NIH) website's full list of rare diseases, which include more than 6,000 diseases; alcoholism, alcohol dependence, and the term addiction are clearly not on the NIH list of rare diseases. The only alcohol related disease listed is alcohol antenatal infection, also known as fetal alcohol syndrome (FAS). FAS is one of the leading known *preventable* causes of mental retardation and birth defects according to the Center for Disease Control and Prevention (CDC) website. This is considered a Spectrum disorder, which can vary on a continuum, and is preventable. FAS has many symptoms present at birth and throughout the development of that child, and is a permanent condition. It only occurs in children whose mothers drink during pregnancy according to the CDC.

Addiction is also absent in the American Psychiatric Associations' Diagnostic and Statistical Manual of Mental Disorders IV (DSM-IV). The term alcoholism is absent as a classification in the DSM-IV. Rather, one can find alcohol dependence and abuse under classification of substance-related disorder. Individuals are classified in this category by behavior, not a physically or mental disease. According to Schaler (2000), "behavior in humans refers to intentional conduct" (p. 18), not a disease, a genetic disposition, or an addictive personality. According to the Saint Jude website,

> The supposed disease's symptoms are only discovered after the consumption of alcohol. The health risk, dangerous behaviors and repercussions only materialize after the alcohol is consumed and not before. In comparison, the diagnosis for cancer comes after symptoms surface or cancerous cells are discovered. There are physically visible anomalies that can be measured. This measurement does not exist with alcoholics" (2005, ¶ 8).

Furthermore, Szasz (2000) looks to the dictionary to define disease as being a "condition of the body, or of some part of organ of the body, in which its functions are disturbed or deranged; a morbid physical condition" (¶ 5). Szasz distinctly separates the mind from the brain, stating that a mind cannot become diseased. Moreover, revolutionary work by Rudolf Virchow (1821-1902) in pathology defines diseases as requiring "an identifiable alteration in bodily tissue, a change in cells of the body, for a disease classification" (Schaler, 2000, p 16). A disease will result in a change in bodily tissue identifiable in a corpse. There is no identified alteration of cells that can be linked to *addiction* only cell changes as the results of chemical use, such as tobacco, alcohol, or other substances (Schaler).

Additionally, if a group of alcoholics are followed for 0 or 40 years, "it is found that alcoholism is not a progressive disease" (Vaillant, 2005, p. 434).

Concerns about the disease approach have been raised in time past by social-learning theorist (Bristow-Braitman, 1995). According to one study, the idea of addiction as a disease reduces the "degree of responsibility clients assumes for their recovery" (Lewis, Dana, & Blevins, 1988, p.12). Fingarette (1988) declares this model came into existence based on cultural values rather than scientific evidence. Despite the research contradicting the disease model, there are still many who hold firm to this model. Flores (1988) argues this model is preferred when working with chemical dependency as it views addiction as a legitimate primary illness and reduces the stigma attached to treating addictions (Coyne & Owen, 1998). It allows the client more dignity to begin the process of changing their behaviors. However, one might still argue, it lacks personal responsibility.

Appendix References

American Medical Association Complete Medical Encyclopedia (2003). American Medical Association online Medical Library. Retrieved at http://medem.com/medlb

Bristow-Braitman, A. (1995). Addiction recovery: 12-step programs and cognitive-behavioral psychology. *Journal of Counseling & Development, 73*, 414-418.

Center for Diseases Control and Prevention (CDC) (2006, May). Fetal Alcohol Spectrum Disorders. Department of Health and Human Services. Retrieved from www.cdc.gov/ncbddd

Conyne, R. K. & Owens, P.C. (1998). Group Psychotherapywith addicted populations: An integration of twelve step and psychodynamic theory. *Group Dynamics, 2*(2), 132-137.

Fingarette, H. (1988). *Heavy drinking: The myth of alcoholism as a disease.* Los Angeles, CA: University of California Press.

Flores, P. (1988). *Group psychotherapy with addicted populations.* New York: Haworth.

Jellinek, E. M. (1946). *Phases in the Drinking History of Alcoholics.* Lake Forest, IL: Whales Tale Press.

Jellinek, E. M. (1952). *The Phases of Alcohol Addiction.* Lake Forest, IL: Whales Tale Press.

Jellinek, E. M. (1960). *The Disease Concept of Alcoholism,* New Haven: College & University Press.

Lewis, J. A., Dana, R. Q., & Blevins, G. A. (1988). *Substance abuse counseling: An individual approach.* Pacific Grove, CA: Brooks/Cole.

Marron, J. T. (1993). The twelve steps. A pathway to recovery. *Primary Care, 20*(1), 107-119.

Merta, R J. (2001, January). Addictions counseling. *Counseling and human Development, 33*(5), 1-26.

National Institute on Drug Abuse (2005). Diagnosis & treatment of drug abuse in family practice: Pathophysiology. Retrieved from the National Institute of Health.

National Institute on Drug Abuse (2006, August 10). NIDA Infofacts: Treatment approaches for drug addiction.

Schaler, J. A. (2000). *Addiction is a choice.* Peru, IL: Open Court.

Szasz, T. (2000, January). Mental disorders are not diseases. *USA Today.* Retrieved from http://www.szasz.com/usatoday.html

Vaillant, G. E. (1983). *The natural history of alcoholism.* Cambridge, MA: Harvard University Press.

References

Alia-Klein, N., Goldstein, R.Z., Tomasi D., Zhang L, Fagin-Jones, S., Telang, F., Wang, G.J., Fowler, J.S., Volkow, N.D. (2007, August). What is in a word? No versus Yes differentially engage the lateral orbitofrontal cortex. *Emotion.*7(3):649-59.

American Psychological Association (2013). *Child sexual abuse; What parents should know.* http://www.apa.org/pi/families/ resources/ child-sexual-abuse

Black, C. (2010, June 4). Understanding the pain of abandonment. The many faces of addiction. *Psychology Today.*

Center for Disease Control and Prevention (2005). *Adverse childhood experiences study: Data and statistics.* Atlanta, GA: Center for Disease Control and Prevention, National Center for Injury Prevention &Control. Retrieved April 1, 2010.

Center for Disease Control and Prevention (2017, January). Impaired Driving Get the Facts. Retrieved from https://www.cdc.gov/ motorvehiclesafety/impaired_driving/impaired-drv_factsheet.html

Cohn, M.A., Fredrickson, B.L., Brown, S.L., Mikels, J.A., & Conway, A.M. (2009, June). Happiness unpacked: Positive emotions increase life satisfaction by building resilience. *Emotion.* 9(3):361-8.

Collinson, T. (2014). Domestic violence and self-esteem, low self-esteem linked to domestic violence. Importance of self-esteem in preventing domestic violence in future generations. *Women Issues.*

Department of Transportation (US), National Highway Traffic Safety Administration (NHTSA). Traffic Safety Facts 2014 data: alcohol-impaired driving. Washington, DC: NHTSA; 2015 [cited 2016 Feb 5]. Available at URL: http://www-nrd. nhtsa.dot. gov/Pubs/812231.pdf

Distilled Spirits Council of the United States (2015). Retrieved from http://www.discus.org/economics/

Domestic Violence Statistics. (2108). https://domesticviolencestatistics. org/

Drug facts: Understanding drug abuse and addiction (revised November 2012). National Institute of Health, National Institute on Drug Abuse. Retrieved from http://www. drugabuse.gov/ publications/drugfacts / understanding-drug-abuse-addiction

Emoto, M. (2004). The Hidden Messages in Water. Hillsboro, OR: Beyond Words.

Erikson, E. H. (1950/1963). *Childhood and society.* Retrieved from https://ncadd.org/

Gottman J. (1993). What *Predicts Divorce?: The Relationship Between*

Marital Processes and Marital Outcomes. Psychology Press.
Harvard Medicine. http://hms.harvard.edu/news/harvard-medicine/chill-fear
Kisley, M.A., Wood, S., Burrows, C.L. (2007, September). Looking at the sunny side of life: age-related change in an event-related potential measure of the negativity bias. *Psychology Science.18*(9):838-43.
Lickerman, A. (2012, September 12). The danger of keeping secrets: When should we keep a secret? What are the risks? *Happiness in this world.*
Losada, M. & Heaphy, E. (2004). The role of positivity and connectivity in the performance of business teams: A nonlinear dynamics model. *American Behavioral Scientist. 47*(6):740–765.
MADD (2015). Statistics. Mothers Against Drunk Driving. www.madd.org
McCoy, Monica L. (2009). Child Abuse and Neglect. Mahwah, NJ: Psychology Press.
National Council on Alcoholism and Drug Dependence. NCADD. (2018). New York: NY.
National Highway Traffic Safety Administration FARS data (2014). http://www nrd.nhtsa.dot. gov/ Pubs/ 812102.pdf
National Highway Traffic Safety Administration (2014). The Economic and Societal Impact Of Motor Vehicle Crashes, 2010. National Highway Traffic Safety Administration, DOT HS 812 013. http://www-nrd.nhtsa.dot.gov/Pubs/812013.pdf
National Institute of Health (2016, July). National Institute on Drug Abuse. Treatment Approaches for Drug Addiction. Retrieved at https://www.drugabuse. gov/publications/drugfacts/ treatment-approaches-drug-addiction
National Institute of Health (2017, April). National Institute on Drug Abuse. Trends & Statistics. Retrieved at https://www.drugabuse.gov/related-topics/trends-statistics
Newberg, A. & Waldman, M. (2012, August 1). The most dangerous word in the world. *Psychology Today.* Sussex.
Office of Women's Health (2018). Effects of Violence Against Women. Department of Health and Human Services. www.Womenshealth.gov.
Parks, A.C., Della, P., Pierce, R.S., Zilca, R., Lyubomirsky, S. (2012, May 28). Pursuing Happiness in Everyday Life: The Characteristics and Behaviors of Online Happiness Seekers. *Emotion.*

Snyder, H.N. (2000, July). *Sexual assault of young children as reported to law enforcement: victim, incident, and offender characteristics.* Retrieved from http://bjs.ojp.usdoj.gov/content/pub/pdf/saycrle.pdf

Stop Violence Against Women. (2018). *Final Report of the Task Force on the Health Effects of Woman Abuse.* (2000). The Effects of Women Abuse. http://www.domesticviolenceinfo.ca/

Substance Abuse and Mental Health Services Administration (SAMHSA). *National Survey of Substance Abuse Treatment Services (N-SSATS): 2013. Data on Substance Abuse Treatment Facilities.* Rockville, MD: Substance Abuse and Mental Health Services Administration; 2014. HHS Publication No. (SMA) 14-489. BHSIS Series S-73.

Substance Abuse and Mental Health Services Administration, Results from the 2012 National Survey on Drug Use and Health: Summary of National Findings, NSDUH Series H-46, HHS Publication No. (SMA) 13-4795. Rockville, MD: Substance Abuse and Mental Health Services Administration, 2013.

Surgeon General's Report (2004). ONDCP. Harwood.

U.S. Bureau of Justice Statistics (1997). *Sex Offenses and Offenders.*

U.S. Department of Health & Human Services. (1995). *1995 Child Maltreatment Survey.* Administration for Children and Families.

U.S. Department of Justice. (2012). *2012 National Crime Victimization Survey.*

Vangelisti, A. L. (1994). Family secrets: Forms, functions, and correlates. *Journal of Social and Personal Relationships, 11,* 113- 135.

WebMD. (2018). Fatal car crashes involving pot have in U.S., study finds. WebMD from HealthDay News (2015). Retrieved from https://www.webmd.com/mental-health/news/20140204/fatal-car-crashes-involving-pot-use-have-tripled-in-us-study-finds#2

Wright, R. (1995). The Moral Animal: Why We Are, the Way We Are: The New Science of Evolutionary Psychology. Vintage.

ABOUT THE AUTHOR

Dr. Keena K. Cowsert is a college professor by day and a ministry leader by night. She has a Master's Degree in Speech Communication with a focus on Organizational Training and Development. Her Doctorate is in Community and Pastoral Counseling. Dr. K teaches public speaking for local colleges in west Florida and online counseling courses for Liberty University's Care and Community Counseling Department.

Dr. K has lead several ministries over the years including: singles, Celebrate Recovery, and women's ministry. She is the founder and director of DK Community (Daughters of the King), a non-profit organization under Galatians 6:2 (www.g62.info). DK Community focuses on women's conferences, Christian art galas, leadership training, discipleship training and Women of Worship nights. Dr. K is a key-note speaker for conferences and other events.

She is passionate about ministry and leading others to a deeper walk in Christ. In her free time, she likes walks on the beach, having coffee with friends and playing with her dogs.

For more information or to schedule Dr. K to speak or bring an event to your area, contact her at:
Email: DKcommunityG62@gmail.com

OTHER WORKS by Dr. K

Pig Moments: God Moments to Remember

Pig Moments gives a fun twist to the God moments in our lives. This book is for anyone who is searching to know God at a deeper level. It will encourage you that you are not isolated in weakness and guide you toward restoration, healing, and wholeness. The many God moments described in this book can occur for anyone seeking Him. Wheeeeeee!!!

Pig Pen: Traces of Mud

God rescues us from sin and the Pig Pen. We do all we can to walk in His calling. Yet, we often find ourselves struggling. Could it be that there are still remnants of mud left from the Pig Pen? This book examines how to wash off all the mud (strongholds, soul ties, generational curses, and word curses,) and allow God to write your new story.

UNMASK: Living Transparently

Unmask: Living Transparently examines the masks that we wear to disguise our weaknesses, protect ourselves from hurt, or to perform for acceptance from others. It examines the defense mechanisms designed to hide the person behind the mask. This book will show how to remove the masks, so you can start to walk in the person that God designed YOU to be.

COMING SOON . . . .

Squeeze Me

Life squeezes us from time-to-time and it is in those times we find out what we are made of. This book looks at what is truly inside of us and what comes out when squeezed. We will examine our own character and the way to walk in God's love and character.

Pig in a Blanket: Wrapped in His Love

This story is a love story! A story of how God comes and wraps us in His love like a warm blanket on a cold day. He will wrap His love around you many different times in your life just to let you feel His love so closely and personally. This journey with piggy will help you examine the times He has personally shown you His love and take you deeper in your walk with Him so you feel that love every day.

www.ingramcontent.com/pod-product-compliance
Lightning Source LLC
LaVergne TN
LVHW051100080426
835508LV00019B/1986